# Spirit Worlds
## Cambodia, The Buddha and The Naga

# Spirit Worlds
## Cambodia, The Buddha and The Naga

Philip Coggan

JOHN BEAUFOY PUBLISHING

# Contents

Front cover photograph: Buddha image in the museum gallery at Angkor Wat;
page 2: Sculpture gallery inside Angkor Wat; page 3: Stone carving at Angkor Wat.

# 1 The Buddha's Tale

*The life of the Buddha is full of marvels. English-language versions usually strip the miracles out, but they can be read as symbols or allegories – for example, the elephant that enters the womb of the Buddha's mother at his conception represents wisdom and majesty. More importantly, the walls and ceilings of Cambodian temples are covered with scenes from the Buddha's life, the Cambodian equivalent of stained glass windows.*

## The Fourth Buddha

According to Buddhist belief there have been many Buddhas (enlightened beings) in the immensely long history of the world, and the world itself has gone through an immense number of cycles in which it is created, destroyed and re-created.

Siddhartha Gautama was the fourth Buddha of the current cycle. His life was practically identical to those of the previous three: divine birth into a princely family, a sheltered upbringing followed by renunciation of the world, the search for enlightenment and its attainment, the teaching ministry, death, and attainment of Nirvana. The life of the fifth will be practically identical again.

There are curious similarities between the life of the Buddha and the life of Jesus as described in the gospels, including an Annunciation, an Immaculate Conception and a Temptation. Scholars believe these are largely coincidental, although it's a fact that in the first millennium the Buddha's story made its way from India to medieval Europe, where he became Saint Josaphat (from Bodhisattva, 'Seeker of Enlightenment') with his feast day on 27 November.

A Bodhisattva is a Buddha-to-be, a heavenly being who has the power to take human form and teach others the way to salvation. The Bodhisattva who became Siddhartha dwelt in the 'heaven of the delighted gods', where a single day is 400 earthly years and a lifespan is 4,000 heavenly years. The gods of all the heavens gathered before him 'with hands joined in adoration' and asked him to be born, so that living beings could learn the path to wisdom and enlightenment.

The Bodhisattva, agreeing that the time had arrived, identified Jambudvipa as the best continent for his birth, Bharat as the best of lands, and Kapilavastu, city of the Sakyas, as the best of cities. He then searched with the all-seeing gaze of a Buddha for a woman who was chaste and modest, of the highest moral standards, who through a hundred thousand reincarnations had refrained from intoxicants, accumulated merit and fulfilled the Ten Perfections. Such a woman he found in Maya, wife of Suddhodana, king of Kapilavastu.

Queen Maya dreamed that the guardian-gods of the four quarters of the universe transported her to the sacred Lake Anotatta on the summit of Mount Meru, whose waters contain the elixir of immortality and will be the last to dry up on the last day of the world. There the heavenly guardians bathed her and led her to a canopied bed strewn with flowers, and the Bodhisattva entered her womb in the form of a white elephant with six tusks. At the moment of the divine conception the ten thousand worlds quaked, the blind saw, the dumb spoke, the lame were made straight, and showers of blossoms fell, and lutes and harps gave forth music without the touch of human fingers.

## The Birth of Siddhartha

Queen Maya awoke and called for her husband, who sent for his Brahmin priests. The Brahmins, when they heard the dream, said: "Be happy, O king, O queen, for a divine being has chosen to be your son. If he lives a life in the world he will become a World Ruler; if he choses to renounce the world, he will become a Buddha."

The pregnancy of the Buddha's mother lasted exactly ten lunar months. When the time for the birth approached she set out for the home of her parents with an escort of companions and servants, and as they passed the Lumbini Garden the queen commanded that her litter be set down so that she could enjoy the perfume of the flowers and shade of the trees.

In the sweet-scented paths she reached up to touch the blossoms of a sal tree, beloved of the god Vishnu, which bent its branch down to her hand. On the full-moon day of the month of Vesak, standing upright and grasping the branch of the sal tree, she gave birth. The gods Indra and Brahma took the child from her side and the infant stood and took seven paces, a lotus springing up at each step. Looking about the entire universe he proclaimed:

> Chief am I in the world,
> Eldest am I in the world,
> Foremost am I in the world,
> This is the final birth,
> There is no more coming to be.

The anniversary of the Buddha's birth, which is also the anniversary of his Enlightenment, death and Nirvana, is called Visak Bochea in Khmer, and is celebrated on the full-moon day of the sixth lunar month, which falls sometimes in April and sometimes in May. Visak Bochea is a time for gaining merit (see *bonn*, page 43). The ceremonies begin with a pre-dawn assembly at the local monastery at which religious flags are raised and hymns chanted in praise of the Buddha, his teaching and the institution of the monkhood. Monks give sermons reminding the faithful of the way to salvation, Buddha images in the shrine halls are washed and offerings of flowers and candles made, alms are given to beggars at the gates, and birds and fish are released. Particularly important and impressive celebrations are held at the former royal city of Oudong, north of Phnom Penh.

## The Great Renunciation

Queen Maya died seven days after the Buddha's birth in order that she should bear no other being in her womb. She was reborn in the heaven of Indra, where she later heard the teaching of the Buddha after his Enlightenment.

The child was given the name Siddhartha, 'He who achieves his goal'. When he was twelve years old the Brahmins revealed to the king that Siddhartha would become a World Ruler if he never saw age, sickness or death. Suddhodana therefore raised his son in seclusion within the palace, knowing nothing of the world, until at the age of 29 he allowed him to venture outside the palace and into the city of Kapilavastu. There the prince saw the true nature of the world in the forms of an old man, a sick man and a corpse being taken to cremation, and came to understand that old age, illness and death were the lot of man. These things caused the prince great distress, but he then came across an ascetic who explained that youth, health and life are transient, and that the way to salvation lies in leaving the world.

Siddhartha returned to the palace, where the king asked what he had seen. Siddhartha said to him: "Can you promise me that my life will not end in death, that sickness will not impair my health, that age will not follow youth, that misfortune will not destroy my prosperity?"

"I cannot promise you these things", his father said.

"If you cannot promise me these things, do not hold me back, O father. The world is a prison, the world is troubled, the world is in a turmoil, the world is a wheel of fire: would that I could bring peace to all men!"

Fearing that his son would leave the palace, Suddhodana set guards on the gates, but the thirty-three gods placed a deep sleep on the city and lifted Siddhartha's horse over the walls. His faithful charioteer, holding the tail of the horse, pleaded with him to remain, but in a steady voice Siddhartha declared: "Until I shall have seen the meaning of life and of death, I shall not return to Kapilavastu."

*The Buddha leaves his father's city.*

## The Middle Way

Cutting his long hair, the sign of a prince, Siddhartha put on the robes of a wanderer and sought enlightenment. From one teacher he learned to discipline his mind and enter the sphere of nothingness, but he did not find supreme enlightenment there. From another he learned how to enter the state that is neither consciousness nor unconsciousness, but this also was not the source of enlightenment. Practising the path of self-denial, he ate only a grain of rice each day, until his ribs beneath his skin were like a dirt road in the monsoon, but this also was not the path to supreme enlightenment.

For five years Siddhartha sought liberation but did not find it. In the sixth year, sitting beneath a bodhi tree by the river, he happened to hear a musician instructing his pupil on a lute, showing how a string which was too tight would not play harmonious music, and nor would a string which was too loose, but only a string strung correctly, neither too tight nor too loose. This was the Middle Way.

Hearing this, Siddhartha left the way of austerity as he had left the luxury of his father's palace.

*Sujata offers food to the Buddha.*

A woman named Sujata, who had recently been blessed with a son by the god of the tree, prepared a thanks-offering of milk-rice, placed it in a golden bowl, and sent her servant-girl ahead to make everything ready. Seeing the Holy One beneath the tree the girl ran back to her mistress, saying, "Mistress, the god himself awaits you!"

Sujata hurried to the tree, where she saw Siddhartha. Realising that this was not a god but a seeker of enlightenment, she bowed and said, "Lord, please accept my offering of milk-rice; may you be successful in obtaining your wish as I have."

Siddhartha broke his fast with the sweet milk-rice Sujata had prepared for the tree-god, and after he had eaten he bathed in the river and took the golden bowl and placed it in the water, saying, "If I am to achieve Buddhahood today, let this bowl float upstream, but if not, let the river carry it downstream."

The golden bowl then floated upstream, keeping to the middle way. When it sank it fell upon the bowls of all the previous Buddhas, and the world rang like a gong so that it woke the *naga* king.

## The Achievement of Enlightenment

In the evening before the full moon of the fourth month Siddhartha sat beneath the bodhi tree and made this resolution: "Let my skin and my bones waste away and my life blood run dry, but I will not rise from this place until I have attained the supreme enlightenment that leads to everlasting happiness."

Desire, craving and fear arose, but he did not allow these to disturb his mind. Breathing in and breathing out he entered into the first jhana, the second jhana, the third jhana and the fourth jhana (meditative states), his mind filled with peace and clarity.

In the first watch of the night he saw his past lives. Recollecting these he said: "In such and such a life I was such and such a name, such was my experience of pleasure and pain, such my life term, and I died; and passing from there, I reappeared elsewhere to such and such a name, such and such an experience of pleasure and pain, such a life term, and died; and passing away from there, I reappeared here."

In the second watch of the night he understood that birth, death and rebirth are suffered by all living beings, whether gods, *asuras*, mankind, animals or hungry ghosts, that all of them are bound by suffering, and that the cause of suffering and rebirth is *kamma* (see page 43).

In the last watch of the night the gods came down from Tavatimsa heaven. Indra and Brahma and Yama worshipped him, *nagas* (serpents) and *garudas* (eagles) attended him, *devatas* burnt incense before him, *apsaras* (mythical dancers) brought him garlands of flowers, and a Brahmin gave him a cushion of grass that transformed into a diamond throne.

Mara ('Illusion'), knowing that the Enlightened One would end his own rule over men, sent his three daughters, Craving, Aversion and Passion, in the form of beautiful girls, to tempt him from the Diamond Throne. Siddhartha unveiled their true hideous forms. Then Mara in anger gathered his army of monsters and demons and prepared to take the Throne by force. The gods and *devatas* were afraid and fled, leaving Siddhartha alone beneath the bodhi tree.

Mara said, "Siddhartha, this Diamond Throne is mine! See who speaks for me!" Mara's army of millions cried out with one voice, "This throne belongs to Illusion! We bear witness!"

Mara challenged Siddhartha: "Who will speak for you?"

Then Siddhartha spoke and said: "Through countless ages my merit has caused all the gods, Indra and Brahma and Yama and all the celestial beings, to pour out blessings on me. This throne is mine by right of merit, and the earth bears witness."

Siddhartha stretched down the fingers of his right hand and touched the earth and a beautiful goddess rose, her breasts bare and her hair heavy with water. The goddess addressed the Holy One, saying: "O Lord! All the offerings of celestial water poured out on your head through countless past aeons have fallen on my hair. I bear witness!"

So saying she stretched out her hair and wrung from it a flood of holy water mightier than the Ganges, with the result that the hordes of Mara were swept away, and Mara bowed down and paid homage.

With Illusion vanquished, Siddhartha attained complete Enlightenment, comprehending the Four Noble Truths and the Noble Eightfold Path (see page 22). Rays of pure light streamed from his body to illuminate the Three Worlds of heaven, earth and hell, transforming the bodhi tree with their brilliance.

## The Seven Weeks After Enlightenment

In the first week the Buddha sat under the bodhi tree, experiencing freedom and mastery. In the second week he stood and meditated on the tree, for which reason it is the custom of all followers of the Way to pay respect to the bodhi tree. In the third week he created a golden bridge and ascended to the heavens, where he taught the Way to the gods.

In the fourth week the Buddha created a jewelled chamber wherein he sat and meditated on the principles that govern all things. At the end of this week his mind was purified and his body emitted six coloured rays of light — yellow for holiness, white for purity, blue for confidence, red for wisdom, orange for the absence of desire and a mixed colour representing the presence of all these noble qualities. (These six make up the Buddhist flag, which is hung outside the prayer hall of every monastery.)

In the fifth week the Buddha said, "There is no me or mine". The three daughters of Mara returned to seduce him, but he continued to meditate, and they departed.

In the sixth week the sky clouded and turned dark, a cold wind blew and heavy rain fell. The king of the *nagas* emerged from his kingdom. Seeing the Enlightened One in deep meditation, the *naga* king coiled his body seven times around the Buddha and raised his five heads to shelter the Salvation of the World.

After seven days the rain stopped and the *naga* changed into the shape of a young Brahmin and reverenced the Buddha. The Buddha said: "Happy is he who hears the Way of Salvation, happy is he who is free from ill-will, who has passed beyond attachment and the senses and all desires, but happiest of all is the ending of the illusion called I Am."

At the end of the seventh week the Buddha, believing that enlightenment was too difficult for humans, thought to enter into Nirvana. The gods Indra and Brahma, fearing that the gift of enlightenment would be denied to mankind, begged him to look on the world and see if there were not some who could benefit from the teaching. The Buddha, gazing on the world with all-seeing eyes of compassion, saw that there were some who could benefit, and agreed to teach.

## The Teaching

On the morning that the seven weeks ended two merchants from foreign lands came, having been informed by the gods that Enlightenment had appeared in this world. They offered rice-cakes and honey, but the Buddha said to them, "The Buddhas do not accept food into their hands; how then can I accept food from your hands?" The gods of the four directions brought crystal bowls, the merchants placed their offerings into the bowls, and the Buddha accepted their offerings and ate. The merchants thus became the first to follow the Buddha.

The merchants asked for a keepsake, and the Enlightened One gave them some hairs from his head. The merchants took the relics to their king, who built the Shwedagon Pagoda in Yangon as their shrine. Later Phnom Penh also acquired relics of the Buddha, enshrined initially in a circular stupa near the Phnom Penh Railway Station and later at Oudom, the old royal capital.

The Buddha rose and went to the Deer Park in Benares (Varanasi), where he preached the first sermon, called Turning the Wheel of Doctrine, to the first five disciples, and afterwards preached the sermon called The Non-Existence of the Soul, on which all five attained Nirvana. This was the beginning of the Sangha, the monkhood.

For the remainder of his earthly life the Buddha travelled and taught the Way to all who wished for release, spending each rainy season in one place. (Today monks enter into a retreat during the rainy season.) Some of those who heard remained in the lay state, while others took the robe. Among these were the Buddha's father, his favourite disciple Ananda, and Mahakasyapa, who lit the Buddha's funeral pyre and led the Sangha after his death.

Rising early, he would brush his teeth and wash his body out of concern for his bodily comfort. When he had done this he would put on his robe and take his bowl and enter the town, sometimes alone, sometimes with others. Soft breezes would sweep the leaves from his path, gentle rain would fall to lay the dust and the clouds would form a canopy to shield him from the sun. With his feet bare and his head shielded he would enter the city gates, six-coloured rays of light would issue from his body, musical instruments would play untouched by human hands and the people would come out in their finest clothing to offer alms and gain merit.

After providing the opportunity for the people to gain merit he would return to the monastery, where he would give guidance to the monks, instructing them to diligently work out their salvation. He would also instruct them in meditation, giving them exercises according to their abilities and attainments.

Following this the monks would retire to the forest to meditate at the foot of the trees, while the Blessed One would rest. Having rested, he would rise refreshed and bathe his limbs with cool water, put on a tunic of red cloth, bind on his girdle, throw his upper robe over his right shoulder, and sit in meditation.

When the time of meditation was ended the monks would come to wait on him. Some would ask questions concerning the *dhamma*, some for exercises in meditation and some for a sermon, and so the Blessed One would complete the first watch of the night.

When the first watch of the night had ended and the monks had departed, the gods would gather in their place to seek wisdom, and so the Blessed One would complete the middle watch of the night.

In the last watch of the night when the gods had departed, the Blessed One would pace up and down to free himself from the discomfort of sitting, then, when his limbs were relaxed, he would lie down, mindful and conscious, to rest his mind, and when his mind was rested he would rise, take his seat and gaze over the world with the eye of a Buddha.

## The Death and Nirvana of the Buddha

The Buddha taught for 45 years, travelling all over northern India, attracting followers and spreading the message of his teaching. In his youth he had seen that old age,

*Death of the Buddha*

illness and death are the common lot of mankind, and he was not immune from these but suffered them like any other man. He died of food poisoning, contracted when he accepted a dish of tainted meat from a follower; he ate the dish despite knowing that the meal was tainted, because the act of offering brought merit to the one who offered.

Attended by monks, gods, nuns and followers, the Buddha lay down between two sal trees and composed himself for death. Ananda, his favourite disciple, wept, but the Buddha said to him: "Do not grieve, Ananda, for that which is born shall perish. You have acquired much merit; exert yourself, and you shall be freed." Turning to the weeping monks he said: "Work out your salvation with diligence!"

These were the last words of the Buddha, as, entering into deep meditation, he passed into Nirvana.

# 2 Secret Maps

*Cambodian religion is a complex blend of Hinduism, Buddhism and animism. Hinduism provides the Khmer with gods, Buddhism with an ethical framework, and animism a rich world of spirits. All three together make up the mandala of Cambodian spiritual life.*

## The Stone Mandala

According to ancient Hindu myth, the world is a disc surrounded by an infinite ocean. The single world-continent was called Jambudvipa ('Island of the Jambu Tree'), and at its centre stood Mount Meru. There in the gardens and palaces of its peak, the gods passed their days in refined pleasure, surrounded by servants as well as musicians, beautiful, bare-breasted *devatas* and graceful, dancing *apsaras*. At Meru's foot was the kingdom of the *asura*-demons, who had once lived on top of Meru with the gods until the gods threw them over the edge on account of their evil behaviour. Beneath Meru were the many circles of hell, the home of the dead and the demons who torment them. Men lived towards the rim of Jambudvipa; the stars, sun and moon circled around Meru's peak, its giant shadow making day and night, as the sun passed behind and in front of it.

(The Buddhist mythical cosmos was identical, except that humans were located on an island south of the main continent; the sacred tree under which the Buddha achieved enlightenment was at its centre; and it was shaped, oddly enough, rather like Tasmania.)

Time passes quickly for humans, but not so for the gods. A *mahakalpa*, one of the longer periods available to the heavenly realms, is measured by the period it would take to empty Lake Anotatta by dipping a blade of grass into it once every hundred years and shaking off a single drop of water. Each *mahakalpa* is made up of four *kalpas*, each *kalpa* will see the lives of a thousand Buddhas, and Siddhartha is the fourth Buddha of the present *kalpa*.

Nine hundred years ago King Suryavarman II built the temple of Angkor Wat. It contains more stone than the Great Pyramid, and is the largest religious structure ever constructed. It is a *mandala*, a symbolic model of the cosmos and the *kalpas*. The *kalpas* are unequal, and so Angkor Wat superimposes them one over another.

The first and longest *kalpa* is represented by the distance from the first step of the causeway over the moat to the geographic centre of the temple (this is the western porch of the second enclosure wall, not the central tower – the mountain is slightly off-centre in the overall plan). The second age, slightly shorter, is the distance from the gate at the western entrance to the bottom step of the central tower; the third, shorter again, runs from the same gate to the wall at the end of the causeway; and the fourth and shortest age is the distance across the moat.

We currently live in the fourth age. This is the worst of all possible worlds. Vice continually increases, morality declines and mankind lives entirely in the physical body. This is the age furthest from the world of the gods, just as the moat is the furthest point from the Meru-mountain, but fortunately it lasts a mere 432,000 years. After the fourth age the universe and the gods will be destroyed, and a new cycle will begin.

Angkor Wat is also a model of cosmic geography. The moat represents the cosmic ocean and the boundary between the real world and the symbolic. The visitor crosses it by the causeway and on the far side passes through a boundary wall representing the mountains dividing the ocean from Jambu. From there a raised stone causeway leads towards the temple, and as the visitor advances the visual experience begins to change from the flat expanse of Jambu to the vertical mass of Meru.

The causeway ends at a cross-shaped stone platform. The temple proper consists of three concentric courtyards on successively higher terraces, each with its own boundary wall and gallery. These are numbered from the centre outward, so the visitor's first gallery is what the guidebooks call the third.

The inner wall of the third (lowest) gallery is filled with a long series of bas-reliefs, arguably the crowning achievement of Khmer art. The scene on the east wall shows the story of Churning of the Ocean of Milk by the gods and *asuras*, one of several Hindu creation myths.

Because the *asuras* were so argumentative Indra, the king of the gods, wished to eject them from Meru, but found himself powerless to do so. In despair the gods turned

*The Churning of the Ocean of Milk.*

to Vishnu, who invented a cunning plan. He proposed to the *asuras* that all the divine beings should join together to churn the ocean and so produce and share the elixir of immortality.

Using a mountain as their churning-rod and the *naga*-king as their rope, the gods and *asuras* began to churn the ocean. The churning produced many wonders. It led the *naga*-king to vomit up a poison so powerful it would have destroyed all creation had the god Shiva not swallowed it; as it was, it caused Shiva's throat to turn blue, for which reason he came to be called Lord Blue Throat. It produced the *apsaras*, who flew upwards to Indra, and Kamadhenu the wish-granting cow, and the moon and conch-shell that became emblems of Vishnu, and also Sura, the argumentative goddess of alcohol with her hair forever in a mess.

Finally the elixir appeared. It was supposed to be shared between the gods and the *asuras*, but Vishnu tricked the *asuras* out of their share by getting them drunk with the help of Sura, then throwing them off the edge of Meru. The *asuras* made their home at the foot of the mountain, below the forests on the slopes guarded by the *garudas* and the *nagas*, and there they remain to this day. They are locked in continual battle with the gods as they

*Devatas guarding the walls of Angkor Wat.*

*Vishnu image from the topmost cell of Angkor Wat, now in the Western Gateway.*

try to regain their place on Meru, but the guardian-gods of the four directions, together with the *nagas* and *garudas*, and the lions who live in the forests forever foil them.

On the second terrace the *devatas* (minor goddesses who act as doorkeepers) begin appearing on the walls, faintly smiling figures standing singly and in groups, quite different from the dancing *apsaras*. More stairs, their extreme steepness emphasizing the approach to the gods, lead to the third terrace, where the roof is decorated with the *nagas*, *garudas* and lions who guard Meru. Four mountain towers surround the innermost courtyard, one at each corner, with a fifth and highest tower in the centre.

At the top of the central tower is a chamber with a shaft in the floor that drops down to a cell at ground level, so that the temple has not four directions – north, south, east, west – but seven, those four plus up, down and centre.

On Suryavarman's death his body was cremated and a portion of his ashes placed in a golden urn in the central chamber. An eight-armed statue of Vishnu – probably the one that now stands in the western entrance – was placed in the chamber at the top. The statue's eyes were opened by Brahmin priests and the king was worshipped there under the name 'He Who Has Gone To Dwell In Vishnu's Realm'.

The great French scholar, Georges Coedes, tells how, in the early part of the 20th century, sophisticated Cambodians refused to believe that their own ancestors had built Angkor, they considered it to have been built by Preah Pisnukar, architect of the gods, for King Preah Ket Mealea. ('Preah' is a prefix used for Buddhas, gods and kings, and the buildings and objects associated with them).

King Preah Ket Mealea was the son of a human mother, but his father was Indra, and when he was twelve years old Indra invited him to visit heaven. There the child gazed in wonder at the jewelled palaces and the gardens filled with flowering trees, and Indra told him that, as he was to rule over Cambodia, the greatest of kingdoms, he would need the grandest of palaces. "Look around you, and if there is any building here that pleases you, tell me and I shall have Preah Pisnukar build it for you."

Ket Mealea was a modest young boy, mindful of his place as both a child and a mortal, and he did not want to offend his father by seeming to set himself on the same level as the gods. And so he declined to copy Indra's own palace, or the dining hall of the Thirty-three Gods, or even one of the pleasure pavilions where the *apsaras* danced. No, instead of these he chose the least of all the buildings in Meru – the palace stables.

Indra, pleased at this display of humility, sent Preah Pisnukar to Earth to oversee the work. As anyone can see, a human lifespan isn't enough time to build Angkor Wat, but Pisnukar moulded the palace out of clay, which he hardened into stone by means of magic.

# Dhamma

Siddhartha Gautama lived in the southern foothills of the Himalayas between Nepal and India, an area he called Bharat. Our Western name, India, comes from the word Sindhu, meaning 'the river', the modern-day Indus River in Pakistan. In ancient times the Persians, close neighbours of the Indians, changed Sindhu to Hindush, and the Greeks adopted this as Indos (the river) and India (the land). The Romans took the name from the Greeks, and modern Europe, with some intermediate steps, inherited it from the Romans. The Arabs took their own name for the country directly from the Persians and called it al-Hind, and 19th century European scholars invented the term Hinduism for the religion of India.

Indian religion was not and is not a single belief. It encompasses the ritual and teachings of the Brahmin priests, the insights of philosophers, the visions of hermits and ascetics, the worship of nature and ancestor spirits, and much else. For this reason modern scholars talk about Brahmanic religion, a term that includes 'Hinduism', (the inverted commas are because of the difficulty of defining the term), cults such as Vaishnavism and Shaivism, which scholars sometimes treat as religions in their own right, Jainism, and many other traditions of which Buddhism is one.

Buddhism is subtle and complex, but it tends to express itself through a number of apparently simple, basic lists. The first of these is the Three Gems:
• Buddha: The aim of human life is to attain enlightenment through the teachings of the Buddha, the Enlightened One;
• Dhamma: Enlightenment can be attained through understanding dhamma, the law of cause and effect that propels the world forward; and
• Sangha: Dhamma can be learnt through the Sangha, the monkhood.

Having grasped the Three Gems, the student moves on to the Four Noble Truths:
• Human life is *dukkha*;
• The cause of *dukkha* is craving;
• There is a way to end *dukkha*;
• The way to end *dukkha* is through the Noble Eightfold Path.

*Dukkha* is often translated as suffering, and it does refer to the ordinary sufferings of life, but *dukkha* is also present in pleasure. Pleasure is transitory, and the ending of pleasure brings suffering, because when pleasure ends we long for it to return.

It is therefore desirable to end craving through the Eightfold Path, whose eight steps and three divisions are:

- Right understanding (wisdom)
- Right intention (wisdom)
- Right speech (virtue)
- Right action (virtue)
- Right means of livelihood (virtue)
- Right mental effort (awareness)
- Right mindfulness (awareness)
- Right concentration (awareness)

The Three Gems tell us that the Sangha is the ideal place from which to grasp the Four Truths and follow the Eightfold Path, but all humans must live virtuous lives.

The way of virtue is set out in the Ten Precepts. These are divided into three groups, formulated as undertakings ('I undertake to…'). The first five are:

1. Refrain from destroying living creatures;
2. Refrain from taking that which is not given;
3. Refrain from sexual misconduct;
4. Refrain from incorrect speech;
5. Refrain from intoxication.

The Five Precepts are supposed to be binding on all Buddhists, and like the Ten Commandments they are easy to grasp but difficult to follow. The first forbids the taking of life – not just human life, but any life at all. Yet fish is the national dish, chicken runs a close second and every villager keeps cows. How are the facts of life to be reconciled with religion?

Sin lies in the act of killing, and to eat meat is not itself against religion. City people buy their fish and chicken in the market, which exempts them from guilt; villagers, closer to the realities of life, say that the fish that swims into the net has not been killed by the fisherman, that the little boys who wring the necks of chickens are too young to be held morally accountable, and that pork and beef come from pigs and cows slaughtered by non-Buddhists such as Chinese and Cham Muslims. Yet despite the casuistry, there is widespread respect for life and for the welfare of animals.

The second and fourth precepts prohibit stealing and lying, and this raises major problems in a country where teachers expect daily 'tea money' from their pupils and firemen will not begin to put out fires until they've been paid. This is endured but not approved of. A young food vendor told an interviewer that a good man is one who neither lies nor cheats and takes only good and legal employment, and that there were not many good men in Cambodia.

The Five Precepts plus three more make the Eight Precepts, mandatory for monks and followed voluntarily by many religiously minded lay people:
6.  Refrain from eating between midday and morning;
7.  Refrain from dancing, music and singing;
8.  Refrain from using high or luxurious seats and beds.
(The last can be interpreted as the avoidance of luxury in general.)

Older Cambodians will often ask each other how many precepts they follow, the five or the eight; there is considerable prestige in following the Eight.

Two final precepts, binding on monks alone, make up the Ten:
9.  To refrain from garlands, perfumes, ointments and other things used to beautify and adorn the person (this precept is broken in a very strange way by boys entering the novitiate for the first time – see page 104);
10. To refrain from handling money.

Integral to *dhamma* is the concept of *karma*, known in Pali, the language of Buddhism, as *kamma*.

Looking at a parallel in the Bible, in the opening verses of the Book of Job, we find that the upright Job is blessed with sons and daughters, and possesses sheep, camels, oxen, donkeys and servants – 'the greatest man among all the people of the East' – and his friends take these blessings as God's reward for a righteous life. When God puts Job's righteousness to the test, taking his sons and daughters, destroying his wealth and afflicting him with boils, his friends advise him to look into his heart and discover what evil he has committed that has caused God to replace blessings with curses. The assumption, in short, is that good fortune in life is God's reward for good deeds, while suffering is the outward sign of inner corruption.

*Kamma* is similar, up to a point. Buddhism agrees that actions determine outcomes – good deeds lead to happiness, bad deeds to suffering. Where it differs markedly is in the absence of God or gods – *kamma* is as impersonal as the law of gravity.

Without reincarnation there can be no *kamma*. For the author of the Book of Job, suffering in this life had to be the outcome of action in this life, or else God is not just (an idea that Job definitely entertains). But when the concept of reincarnation is linked to the workings of *kamma*, it becomes clear, or at least plausible, that the consequences of good and bad deeds can be played out over countless lives.

The basis of reincarnation is the nature of the self, a concept by no means so universally obvious as might be supposed. In India in the Buddha's time it was generally agreed that the self was an irreducible and permanent essence, called the *atman*. The *atman* was eternal and unchanging and continued from one life to the next, the individual expression of, and ultimately identical with, the source of the universe. That which was reincarnated was therefore eternal and unchanging, although capable of realising its identity with the universal.

The Buddha challenged this. The *atman*, he taught, arises when the consciousness forms an impression of its existence as a separate self. But this sense of uniqueness is a misapprehension, formed on the evidence of the senses, which perceive only the flow of impermanent impressions. This illusion of uniqueness is the cause of craving, and thereby of *dukkha*, which keeps us tied to *samsara*, the wheel of birth, death and rebirth.

It follows that the *atman* is not immortal. Even the gods, although their lives are immensely long, millions and millions of years, are subject to the workings of rebirth and are not immortal. The ultimate goal is not to be reborn, not even as a god, but to end the illusion of self and reach the state of nirvana.

Nirvana (*nirvana* in Pali, *niban* in Khmer) means blowing out, as in extinguishing a candle. We are attached to the things of this world through our senses, which perceive the world as real and ourselves (our 'selves') as incomplete. Attachment leads to craving, to fearing the loss of those things we possess, to wanting those things we don't possess, and so we remain trapped in a state of incompletion. Being ignorant of the means of escape we remain attached, and the world continues to be *dukkha*. To reach nirvana is to put out the fires of attachment, lust and ignorance, and to end illusion. The attainment of nirvana is the highest goal of human life, and the aim of the Buddha's teaching.

## The World of Animism

Animism is the belief that the entire world, human and non-human, living and non-living, forms a single spiritual whole. Just as people have souls, so do animals; and just as humans and animals are inhabited by a living spirit ('animated'), so too are streams and hills and every other natural object.

An immense range and variety of spirits inhabit the Khmer universe. The following is a brief overview of a few of the more important ones.

- *Preah Phum*: the spirit of the village as a whole, including its houses, ponds, cattle pastures, mango groves, irrigation canals and rice fields. The *preah phum* of a particular village has no name, but has to be treated with respect if the village is to enjoy good health and avoid disasters, such as drought and epidemics. The *preah phum* has to be called up when a village is first established or re-established after some disaster.
- *Neak Ta*: There are three types of *neak ta*, the 'wild' *neak ta* of the wilderness whose permission has to be sought when entering their territory, the 'village' *neak ta* who look after a specific village, and the 'great' *neak ta* who look after whole regions.
- *Arak*: Wild spirits who inhabit the village fields and edges.
- *Boramey*: A class of spirits who wish to help humans. Some of the *boramey* are also *neak ta*, but not all.
- *Meba*: The family ancestors.
- Various spirits of trees, ponds, hills and other natural features, and also such entities as the wind and clouds.

The spirits can be contacted by human intermediaries, called *kru*, from the Sankrit word *guru*, and meaning master or teacher. There are many types of *kru*, including *kru khmer*, who are healers and understand herbs, leaves and roots, and the spells and rituals that make them effective, *kru arak*, who contact the village *arak*, and *kru boramey*, who are in contact with the powerful *boramey* spirits.

Not all spirits are helpful. The village is also home to malevolent spirits who must be avoided or placated. These attract the attention of sorcerers, who harness them to cause sickness or harm to their enemies. Ordinary villagers fear sorcerers, and good *krus* (the vast majority) despise them, but everyone knows they exist.

The spirit world explains and controls fertility and rebirth, death and the dead, dreams and consciousness, sickness and health. It is linked to myth, visions and mysticism. It is deeply magical, and also deeply moral. Take, for example, the *koan krak*. This amulet is created by cutting open a pregnant woman and taking her unborn child. The fetus, worn in a sack round the neck, speaks to its 'father' (its owner) in dreams, warning him of danger and of the plots of his enemies, turning aside attacks, even allowing him to become invisible. It sounds horrific, and yet its function is entirely protective. If the owner tries to use it to harm others, it will fall silent, and quite possibly turn against him.

# 3 Tales from the Shadow World

*How do Cambodians live their spiritual lives? A village elder talks about the spirit of his village, a husband tells about his difficulties with grandmothers both living and yet to be born, a farmer talks about the spirits and demons, and a girl from Phnom Penh tells how the spirits are present in her life.*

## The Grandfather's Tale

The *neak ta* are the single most important class of supernatural beings in Cambodia. One expert defines them as generic spirits of trees, paddies, streams and other natural features, another as the symbolic representation of the land and its fertility, the spiritual first person, real or mythical, to cultivate the soil in that place. Their name suggests ancestors – but no living human is related to them and the name signifies no more than that, through the *neak ta*, the village becomes a family.

The *neak ta* are the owners of the land, and humans are trespassers. They are not inherently benign. Hunters and travellers entering forests and wilderness areas must placate them and ask permission to pass through their territory; villagers wishing to open up new fields for cultivation, transforming inhospitable 'prey' into habitable land – 'srok' – must approach them with humility and go through the proper rituals.

*Neak ta* are the only spirits to be represented by an image. This can be a statue of a man or woman, a Shiva-linga salvaged from an Angkorean temple, a stone or a termite mound representing the earth in the process of self-transformation. (There's a well-known example of a termite mound *neak ta* in one of the outer galleries at Angkor Wat.) They are always associated with fertility, both of the fields and of the people. Some have names but most are known by a title – *neak ta* of the bodhi tree, *neak ta* of the village. They take a lively interest in village life, and every *neak ta* has an annual festival when the entire village gathers at his shrine for a feast in his honour.

Prek Luong village has a strange name, because a *prek* is a canal or lake, and *luong* is a word for the royal family. There's a local legend about a prince with a magic hand, who fled the royal capital at Oudong and built a palace here, then with his magic hand he dug a canal to link his palace to the river. The legend also says that the prince had a wicked uncle who hunted him down and killed him. According to non-magical history something rather similar did happen in this area several centuries ago.

Like many village-level *neak ta*, the resident spirit of Prek Luong has no name. He was originally called Neak Ta Me Chas Srok, 'Neak Ta of the Old Village', in which form he was represented by a large stone which sadly no longer exists. I suspect it may have been an artefact from an earlier age, as Prek Luong is on the banks of the Mekong and there's nothing here but silt, but the Khmer Rouge took it away and nobody knows what happened to it.

The man who told me this was Ta Krit ('Grandfather Krit'), aged 81, a native of Prek Luong. In his youth Ta Krit had been a communist, which helped him survive the Khmer Rouge and he became commune chief in 1979. He kept that position for the next 30 years, which bespeaks a sharp political mind.

One of his very first, self-appointed tasks was to restore the lost *neak ta* of Prek Luong. How to do this? He noticed that the village cows were avoiding three succulent young banana saplings growing in a field on the edge the village. Upon investigating, he found a self-sown bodhi tree growing between and protected by the plants. Under his direction the villagers built a small wooden shrine near the tree and invited their *neak ta* to take up residence in his new home. After three decades the tree has grown large, and the spirit is now called Neak Ta Dam Po, the Bodhi Tree Ancestor.

Prek Luong is a rather prosperous village, and several years ago Ta Krit had the wooden shrine replaced with a more substantial structure of cement and tiles. A little after that he commissioned a statue for the shrine to deter the local children from using it for their games – this would be bound to offend the *neak ta*, and he didn't want the spirit to punish innocent infants for their play.

A *sala chan*, or dining hall for monks, has also been built under the bodhi tree near the shrine, and each February the four hamlets making up the village gather here for a harvest festival called 'Walking the Fields'. The festival has the practical purpose of

*Children play in the* sala chan, *Prek Luong village.*

reminding everyone of the village boundaries and fields, and the spiritual one of asking the *neak ta* for his blessing of continued fertility.

Ta Krit told me that Neak Ta Dam Po is a strong spirit, who always grants his people their requests. These are for the usual things – children, good health and lucky lottery ticket numbers. As an example of Dam Po's power and benevolence, Ta Krit quoted his own daughter's wedding: the monsoon had lingered that year and black clouds were gathering as the day arrived, but Ta Krit prayed to Dam Po, the sky cleared and the wedding was a great success. Ta Krit himself has never been sick in all his 81 years, and he puts this down to the goodness of the village patron.

Neak Ta Dam Po loves those who are honest, who speak the truth and keep their word, whose hearts are pure, who never harm others and are not greedy. But he must be treated with proper respect. He is happy to share the fruits from the mango trees that grow in his compound, but those who want to pick them must ask permission first. Similarly the children are welcome to play in the *sala chan*, but not in the *neak ta*'s shrine, and they must not throw stones, or use bad language in his presence.

Those who anger him he punishes with illness. If someone in the village falls ill and the illness fails to respond to treatment in the clinic, Dam Po must be consulted through the *kru* to find out what spirit has been angered, and why.

The statue of Neak Ta Dam Po shows a strongly-built middle aged man, squatting, with a clenched hand resting on one raised knee. This is a classic pose I've noticed in many male *neak ta*, though I don't think anyone has ever done a study of *neak ta* iconography. I'm told it's the pose of all lower spirit-beings. The other hand hangs downward with the palm turned outward in the generosity *mudra*. (The *mudras* are a set of stylized symbolic gestures for Buddha images – right hand raised with palm outward means dispelling fear, both hands cupped in the lap means meditation, and so on.)

The statue is the work of a village artist, Hang Sovann, who also decorated the *sala chan*. I later met Hang Sovann, who told me that when he was young and poor he saw the *neak ta* quite often in dreams and waking, which is how he knew what he looked like. The *neak ta* told him then that one day he would be rich and asked to be remembered when the time came, and the statue is his thanks to the spirit.

There's a second *neak ta* in the village, because while Neak Ta Dam Po is the village ancestor there's another one for the monastery. His name is Neak Ta Kuy, which I was told is Chinese but otherwise has no meaning. His shrine is almost as large as Neak Ta Dam Po's, but instead of a Khmer statue it has some Chinese figurines and a board with Chinese characters.

Neak Ta Kuy, like Neak Ta Dam Po, will punish anyone who breaches the rules of good behaviour, such as using bad language or urinating within the temple boundary. His authority is limited to the monastery, but nevertheless he fulfils an important function as the village representative in its corporate dealings with the outside world – Neak Ta Dam Po could perhaps equate to Prek Luong's spirit Prime Minister, and Neak Ta Kuy its Minister for Foreign Affairs.

The day of my visit was two weeks before the annual Boat Race Festival, three days of boat races that take place opposite the Royal Palace in Phnom Penh. Not only in Phnom Penh – other races are held all over the country – but the Phnom Penh event is by far the most important, presided over by the king himself in front of millions of spectators. The boats represent villages, and for most of the year they're stored in boat-sheds in the village monasteries under the eye of the temple *neak ta*. An offering-ceremony for the Prek Luong boat was just ending when I arrived, Neak Ta Kuy being asked to lend his strength to the rowers. Most of the male village seemed to be there.

Prek Luong's boat, like all the others, was made from a single tree. The spirit that

*Neak Ta Dam Po.*

inhabited the tree was asked for her permission to cut it down, then asked to remain with the boat to fend off the spirits of rival boats. The spirit is a *bray*, a woman who died in childbirth. Like all *bray* she is evil, and in her malevolence she causes childlessness and miscarriages for any pregnant woman who crosses in front of the boat. Hence there were no women present at the ceremony at Neak Ta Kuy's shrine.

Because of her evil nature the *bray* is the most powerful of spirits. Most of the time she's to be feared and shunned, but the monastery *neak ta* can tame her and turn her into a servant of the Buddha. So on the morning of the first day of the races, with the help of a *pinpeat* orchestra of xylophones and reeds (or perhaps a CD, since *pinpeat* orchestras are expensive), rituals will be performed and the prettiest girls in the village will dance like *apsaras* to please the spirit.

Prek Luong's boat, with the help of its *neak ta* and *bray*, wins every race it enters. As the custodian of the boat told me, "When they see the black boat of Prek Luong on the river their knees turn to jelly and they cannot contain their water!"

## The Grandmother's Tale

My friend Socheat, who works as a marketing executive, and his wife, an accountant, are expecting their first baby. As is usual all over the world, nobody thinks this coming event more important than does the mother's mother, and nobody is a stronger champion of tradition.

The *kru* has already pronounced on the sex of the unborn (a girl); the ultrasound at the clinic was merely the confirmation of a known fact. But now there's a problem: Socheat's wife feels Socheat isn't spending enough time with her. Instead of hurrying home after work each day he goes out with his friends. Doesn't he care? They've quarrelled. Not seriously, but they've had words. Socheat, as a modern and scientific Cambodian, says his wife has become unreasonable; the baby, he says, is making her short-tempered. He puts it down to hormones.

Socheat's wife told her mother, and her mother took her to the *kru*. The *kru* told them that the baby is indeed the cause of the problem. It's the reincarnated spirit of Socheat's grandmother. He should listen to his grandmother, and spend more time with his wife.

Family is a fundamental pillar of Cambodian society. Family, however, does not have the same meaning that it has in the West, as it includes the ancestors, the *meba*. This is common enough in animistic societies, but in Cambodia the belief in reincarnation adds a twist: your *meba* are not, as might be expected, your biological ancestors, but your ancestors by reincarnation. This means that your *meba* mothers are all the mothers from your previous lives. The distinction is perhaps academic, as grandparents commonly reincarnate as their own grandchildren and great-grandchildren. Prime Minister Hun Sen, for example, told his official biographers that he believes his granddaughter is the reincarnation of his mother – "whenever anyone my mother knew comes into the house, the infant looks and smiles at that person".

The *meba* are closely involved in ongoing family affairs. At weddings they are asked to bless the future life of the couple and to prevent fights between inebriated guests, and when the newly wedded wife falls pregnant she informs the *meba* that an addition to the family is expected, and again when the baby arrives.

The *meba* have strict moral standards. They punish girls (but not boys) who engage in pre-marital sex, and if someone falls sick without reason, or if an illness fails to respond to treatment, it will be necessary to find out whether illicit sex is the cause. Conversely, they have sympathy for the young and can cause a family member to fall sick if parents forbid a love-match; this sickness will not lift until the parents ask the *meba* for forgiveness.

Early childhood in Cambodia is idyllic. Infants are fussed over, toddlers are indulged. This continues until the next child comes and the focus switches to the new arrival. With each new sibling, the first child is pushed into greater and greater responsibility, often beginning at a very early age.

Children owe their parents a debt that can never be repaid. The debt is the gift of life itself, but also the fact that the parents, especially the mother, have given them nurture and morality. The Buddhist scriptures list many types of sin, but there is none so great as filial ingratitude.

The mother is the source of nurture and love, but also of punishment and betrayal as early indulgence is progressively withdrawn. The way to please the mother is through obedience, which brings a return of love and approval.

Fathers seem absent from the Khmer psyche, or at least not nearly so highly valued as mothers. In place of the father, oddly enough, the grandfather seems to assume the role of parental nurturer. The Khmer term for what in the West would be termed the family name is *chmoh chi-ta*, literally 'name of grandfather'. Navy Phim, explaining this in her *Reflections on a Khmer Soul*, says:

"My last name (actually her first name, since the family name comes first in traditional usage) would be the name of my grandfather on my father's side, and the last name (i.e., family name) of my children would be the last name (family name) of my husband's father. At least, this is how it works in my parents' province, Battambang."

In a society where there are essentially no bonds between people apart from the family, fictive familial relations are created. One's elders are always referred to by polite family terms, even when not actually family. Anyone of more of less the same age is called *bong*, meaning big brother or big sister (Khmer doesn't distinguish the two), those who are appreciably younger are *oun*, meaning younger family member, and elders are *daun chi* or *ta chi*, grandmother or grandfather.

## The Farmer's Tale

Eng Sok, of Svay Chrum village in Kandal province, is 71 years old and has been a farmer all his life. He sits on a blue plastic chair in the front yard of his house to answer questions about those inhabitants of his village who are neither human nor animal. Some are spirits, some are ghosts and some are monsters. Some are benign, but most are not.

First come the dead, who exist somewhere on the border of the natural world. The dead cannot easily give up the world of the living; they have to be eased into the spirit world gradually. For this reason, after death and cremation, their ashes and bone fragments are collected and kept in the family home. (Eng Sok didn't mention it, but there's a new fashion for constructing a large shrine in front of the house for the storage of ashes, with a broad plinth where prayers can be made and offerings left.) But the elderly departed are crotchety, disliking noise and liable to be annoyed by children, and children in turn are likely to be frightened by the dead, therefore the ashes are taken to a monastery after a certain period.

Next come the spirits (see also chapter 8).

The *mrieng kongveal* are child-spirits who live in the trees around the village. The *mrieng kongveal* are naked, but they wrap a red cloth around their heads, or else shave their hair leaving a lock at the forehead, in the traditional way of human children. Like many villagers, Eng Sok keeps a shrine for the *mrieng kongveal* under his house, because when they see human children in a house they come and play with them. Eng Sok and the rest of the villagers know these spirits are real because they see their own children and grandchildren talking and laughing and playing games with them, although they're invisible to adult eyes. Sometimes they play too roughly, in which case the human child will get a fever or cough. Then the parents will offer food and water and sweets to the *mrieng kongveal* and ask them to remember that human children are more delicate than spirits.

A house can do without a shrine for the *mrieng kongveal*, but not without one for the *chumneang pteah*, the protective spirit of the house. The spirit lives in one of the house

THE FARMER'S TALE | 35

pillars, and this is the best place for its shrine if people can discover which pillar it is. If this is not possible, then any pillar will do, but it should always face the door. The house spirit will bring prosperity and happiness to the family, but the shrine has to be kept clean and incense should be burned, and offerings made on the full moon, dark moon and quarter moon days of each lunar month.

Eng Sok rarely sees spirits, but once when he was walking home in the evening, he saw a woman standing on the roof of his house. The woman launched herself into the air and flew towards him, vanishing at the last moment, and he knew at once this was the *chumneang pteah*.

Finally there are the *tevoda*. These spirits have their shrine set on a pillar outside the house, and their role is to watch over the house and its inhabitants, guarding them from the dark forces that inhabit the village.

These three are the household spirits. After them come the spirits of the village. The *arak* are spirits of natural features (*arak* of the forests, *arak* of the water, etc). Some anthropologists describe them as ancestor-spirits, but Eng Sok didn't say this. They are sometimes willing to help humans, but are unpredictable, potentially dangerous and should be approached only by an experienced *kru*. Eng Sok is not sure he believes in them, but he keeps an open mind because of the testimony of people from the village who have been cured of illness by the *arak* after the hospital was unable to help. Farmers working in the fields always share their food with them, a little each of whatever they have, placed on a banana leaf on the ground, but under no circumstances should an offering to the *arak* be placed on the dirt.

Prek Luong's *kru arak* is 90 and still active, but no successor has been trained; in another village I was told that the local *kru arak* had died about ten years ago and no new one had come forward. According to the anthropologists who study these things, the institution of the *kru arak* seems to be dying out in Cambodia.

The *mrieng kongveal*, the *chumneang pteah* and the *tevoda* are friends to humans, although they shouldn't be crossed, and the *arak* are neutral but potentially helpful. Utterly different is the *bray*, who attacks women at the hour of childbirth to kill them and their babies. The *bray* manifests at night as a large green light, and Eng Sok and other villagers have seen it flying from tree to tree or coming from nowhere to land in a tamarind or bodhi tree, both, like the koki tree, charged with supernatural power. The villagers never allow a bodhi tree to grow in a house-yard, and only monks or kings would plant a koki tree, but tamarind trees are useful and are grown by everyone despite the danger. If a villager finds a *bray* in his tamarind he can get rid of it by hammering a nail into the trunk, but if this fails the tree has to be destroyed.

Alongside the evil spirits are human monsters. The best-known is the *arp*, a malevolent being found under various names in every country in Southeast Asia regardless of religion, language or ethnicity. In Thailand she's the *krasue*, in Malaysia and Indonesia the *penanggalan*, and in the Philippines the *mananaggal*. The word is frequently translated as vampire, but she's really quite different. Eng Sok says she's a woman who learnt magic in order to have a 'charming face' that no man can fail to fall in love with, a woman addicted to pleasure who wants to stay young forever. In her human form she can be recognized by her sunken red eyes, because she sleeps by day, when good housewives are caring for house and family. The home of an *arp* can be instantly recognised because she's a slovenly housekeeper, her house will be dirty and untidy, trash scattered across the house-yard, nothing done properly and nothing in its proper place.

By day the *arp* is human in appearance, but at night her head detaches from her body and flies around, viscera dangling from the neck, spreading disease in the entrails of sleepers by means of her immensely long tongue. She is the cause of nightmares, abortions and infertility, she feeds on kitchen slops under houses and on the corpses of dead dogs left on the street. She manifests herself as a red light, and farmers going out early to the rice paddies sometimes come across her before the sun rises, chasing her breakfast of frogs across the fields. She has a particular appetite for the afterbirth of newborn babies, and for this reason a pregnant woman should place protective amulets at the entrance to her bedroom and cactus or thorns under the bed when giving birth to keep the monster at bay.

Eng Sok has never seen an *arp* himself, but he heard this story about a man who discovered that his wife was an *arp*. The man woke very early one morning to find his wife's body beside him in the bed, minus the head. He concealed the body then hid and waited, and, sure enough, at dawn his wife's head returned, innards dangling down from its neck. Enraged to find her body no longer lying where she had left it she flew around the house like a whirlwind, and when she it found it the two parts joined together and became the man's wife again.

(Eng Sok's story of the man and his *arp*-wife ended on a cliff-hanger, and I never found out what happened next. The *arp* is by far the most popular monster in Cambodia; the first film made after the fall of the Khmer Rouge was a horror movie called *Kon Aeuy Madai Arp*, 'My Mother is an Arp'. Many more have followed.)

Then there are rare monsters such as the *smir*, or were-tiger. A woman anoints herself with corpse-oil (grease from the body-fat of a human corpse) over which appropriate incantations have been made, runs into the forest, joins the tigers, grows fur, and becomes a tiger herself. Eng Sok says has never heard of such a thing happening in Svay Chrum.

Finally there are the ghosts. Ghosts which have gone to the afterworld are almost part of the community: once a year they come back to the village to look for their living relatives, and a feast is organized for them. If this is done they're quite harmless, though if neglected they can cause illness and misfortune. But some ghosts have not found their way to hell and stay around the village to frighten people. A haunting ghost appears with bulging eyes, a lolling tongue and wild hair. If you want to see a haunt, paint crosses on your heels and walk backwards. They don't cause much real trouble and can be laid to rest with the help of monks or a *kru*.

In a countryside populated by unseen presences, most of them malign or potentially so, humans must do what they can to protect themselves. Bottles of red water can be hung from the house eaves to distract the *arp*; in some places the villagers erect human-sized scare-crows called *ting mong*, armed with swords and guns, to frighten off evil spirits. In 2012 in Tmey, a village in Banteay Meanchey province near the Thai border, this was the work of bands of little boys warding off an epidemic that seemed to target children; some adults, if questioned, would laugh and say they put them up because the children like them or demand them, but others would not live in a house with no protection.

Then there are sorcerers. Respectable *kru* help people. The *kru khmer* heals broken bones (broken bones are one of the major hazards of village life), the *kru arak* finds lost cattle, the *kru boramey* contacts the dead. All these work for good. But sometimes people's wants are on the borderline. What to do for a woman whose husband has run off with another woman? So harsh to tell her you won't help when you know you can. Or the policeman who wants a talisman or tattoo to protect his life? These involve conjuring up powerful spirits. The line is blurry, but most *kru* are careful not to cross it. They are always aware of the primary teaching of the Buddha, which is to do no harm.

True black magic exists, everyone knows it. The most horrific forms involve nails from coffins, oil distilled from corpses and foetuses torn from the wombs of living women. These confer powers on the owner, the dead bound to the will of the living. The black magician can cause razor blades and needles to enter the body of an enemy, or a buffalo skin that will swell up in the stomach. The person so attacked becomes ill, and will die if not helped by white magic.

Every year, in villages round the country, Cambodians are killed by their neighbours for practising black magic. Quite often this will be a previously 'good' *kru* who is suspected of having turned to the dark side. Often their livers are eaten, a practice found throughout Southeast Asia. Very seldom are the victims actually guilty of even attempting to cause harm.

"According to Buddhist principles there is no such thing as black magic", says Venerable Yos Hut Khemacaro of Wat Langka. "If a person goes to see a monk and really believes they have been cursed by black magic, the monk should explain to the person that black magic does not exist. If people have a problem and they have nowhere to go, they will turn to the *kru khmers*, but if there is a hospital, they will go to the hospital. When people feel helpless they turn to magic, but if they have access to proper services, there will no longer be such beliefs."

## The Maiden's Tale

While Eng Sok lives with the spirits, Chanthy represents the opposite situation: the spirits live with her.

Chanthy is 26 years old, the eldest of four children, and grew up in Ponhea Leu near Oudong. When she was growing up her village was a rural area, but it's long since been absorbed into the outer fringes of the Phnom Penh urban area. There was nothing remarkable about her childhood. Her father deserted her mother when she was about seven or eight, but he continued to live nearby with his new wife, remained friendly with Chanthy's mother and saw his children every day.

One day her mother cooked snake for the family. Chanthy got very, very sick, although nobody else in the family was affected, and that night a spirit came and tried to drag her out from the house. Next day her mother made an offering to the spirit and asked it not to punish her daughter because she hadn't known the food was snake and Chanthy promised never to eat snake again. This was the first time she and her family knew about the spirit.

The next episode was when she was around 15 or 16. It was about 11 in the morning and the family were sitting in the house when Chanthy saw a huge snake in the room, looking at her. Nobody else saw it, and her mother said it was not possible for a snake to be there. Her mother took her to a *kru* who explained that this was a spirit, saying that Chanthy and her mother should burn incense and ask it not to frighten her.

After this the serpent-spirit came to visit her at night in dreams. She and the serpent would sleep together, and she would ride on the friendly *naga*'s back to its palace, where there were many serpents who respected her serpent as king of the *nagas*.

Chanthy's neighbours asked her to be their *kru*. She asked the serpent-spirit for advice, and the spirit gave her a choice, to become a *kru* or to become a *neak kanseul*, ('a person who is serious about religion') for three years. Being a *neak kanseul* would mean she would have to follow the five precepts, and obey the spirit – for example, if she wanted to go somewhere and spirit said no, she would have to take the consequences if she disobeyed. Being a *neak kanseul* was difficult, but she chose this because she felt she wasn't ready to be a *kru*.

Chanthy left school at 18 and went to work in one of the new garment factories around Ponhea Leu. She quit after four days: "I was standing all day and my ankles and legs were swollen and I was exhausted." She stayed at home for a while after that, but when she was 20 she moved to Phnom Penh to sell clothing at Sorya Mall, which had just opened. Her salary was $80 a month and she paid $30 a month for her room which left only $50 a month to live on, but she brought her two younger sisters with her who also found work and so the three of them weren't badly off.

The serpent-spirit came with her to Phnom Penh. After a year or so her sisters went back to Ponhea Leu, but the serpent-spirit stayed and is still with her. She's very glad to have the *naga* with her, because it looks after her and tells her what will happen and what decisions to make. She burns incense for it every day, and offers it food and water, and asks it to continue to support her.

She also has the *chumneang pteah*. Unlike the serpent, the *chumneang* spirit appears when she's awake as well as in dreams. What she sees is not a man, but something like a shadow of a man, tall and dark skinned. She sees it almost every week, and especially before the holy days of each month. (Chanthy is talking about the Khmer lunar month; the holy days are the new moon day, the full moon day and the two half-moon days.)

The *chumneang pteah* protects the house. One night she heard a voice telling her to wake up and when she woke up she heard a burglar trying to break in. She screamed and the burglar ran away, but he left the stick he'd been using to try to break the lock. She was too scared to remember to thank the spirit but called her boyfriend and her friends who all came and kept her company for the rest of the night.

Sometimes she asks the *chumneang pteah* for favours. On one occasion she needed rent money and she told the spirit, "If you don't help me I'll have to leave the house and leave you", and the next day someone who owed her money paid her back. She's asked the spirit to see that a job application was successful and it was, and she's asked to meet someone important to her and she did. Everything she asks from the *chumneang pteah* comes true.

She has a shrine for the *chumneang pteah* and one for the *naga*. She burns incense and offers bananas, fruits, jasmine flowers and water to both, and these must be refreshed every holy day. The *chumneang pteah* tells her what he wants to eat or drink, and she's always very careful to follow his wishes. Once he asked her not to walk round the apartment naked after her shower, even though she was otherwise alone, because it embarrassed him. If she hasn't seen the *chumneang pteah* for a while she can ask him on the holy day, and she will see him.

There's another spirit too. Recently Chanthy was breaking up with her boyfriend. She was hurting badly, so badly she thought of suicide. She stood in her kitchen looking at the knife on the table, but when she stretched out her hand a spirit grabbed her wrist. "The spirit told me that every problem has a solution and if I stay alive he will stay with me forever and help me and find me a boyfriend who will love me, but if I kill myself he will never help me again."

This spirit is a *pralung*, a human soul. Chanthy believes the *pralung* must have had a sad life as it seems to understand so well how she felt, and wants to help humans in this world. The next day she thought of suicide again, but she remembered the *pralung* and gave up the idea. Three or four days later she got back together with her boyfriend. That night the *pralung* came to her and told her it had spoken the truth, it had promised to help and it had helped, and she should never kill herself, because a person who kills herself is lost forever.

# 4 *Kamm* and *Bonn*

*Cambodian Buddhism is not quite as the textbooks describe. The words* kamm *and* bonn *are Khmer, and although the concepts behind them derive from Buddhism they take on a subtly different meaning in everyday life, bound up with ideas of reincarnation, social status, and power and its sources.*

## The Man of *Kamm*'s Tale

Vannak is 27 and comes from Prey Veng province. Like so many others he arrived in the city in his early teens to seek his fortune, but never found it. His mother came too, and became a seller of lotus flowers at the riverside shrine of Preah Ang Doun Kar. Now she's dying. Her stomach has become hugely distended, as if she's expecting a child, but as Vannak points out she's in her sixties, she's lived away from her husband, Vannak's father, for 15 years, and in any case he died last year.

Vannak, like a large number of young men in Phnom Penh, exists in a state of permanent debt: he borrows from his friends when he has no money, and lends to them when he does. So he borrowed some money and took his mother to the doctor, and the doctor said she has water on the stomach. Several conditions, most notably liver cancer, can cause the liver to shut down, which causes fluid retention and subsequent bloating of the abdomen.

The doctor recommended the usual raft of antibiotics that get prescribed for every ailment from piles to TB. These are expensive, and I hesitate to suggest collusion

between doctors and pharmacists, but medical costs are the single biggest cause of poor Cambodians sliding into outright destitution. Vannak borrowed some more and bought them, but his mother's condition failed to improve. So he took her to a respected monk, who prescribed amulets. These also cost money, but less than the antibiotics. More usefully, the monk told Vannak that the span of each life is limited. At a certain point, one must put one's accounts in order.

Vannak does not blame himself for the death of his father or the approaching death of his mother. These things are natural and to be expected, as the monk reminded him. And caring for his mother brings merit. Nevertheless, his soul is clearly clogged with *kamm*. So having done all he can for his mother, he intends to go to the monk again, this time for himself. "I want my *kamm* out and my good luck in."

*Kamm* is colloquial Khmer for *kamma*, the Pali equivalent of *karma*. *Karma* and *kamma* mean the same thing, intentional acts, which include thoughts and words as well as deeds. The Buddha said *kamma* was the impulse of the mind preceding and causing visible action.

The meaning of *kamm* is slightly different. *Kamm*, for Vannak, is not a mental impulse but a store of evil, hanging over his head like a storm cloud, letting loose the lightning strikes of bad luck. In the West there's nothing you can do about bad luck, it just happens, and if the rabbit's foot didn't help the rabbit it probably won't help you. In Cambodia both Buddhism and animism hold that bad luck is not random, and it's therefore up to the individual to look after his *kamm* as much as his bodily health.

The desirable opposite of *kamm*, the equivalent of spiritual good health, is *bonn*, meaning merit. *Bonn* is the product of deliberate merit-making acts, the best of which is to become a monk. Short of that, layfolk can gain merit by giving alms. Monks do not beg, they provide laypersons with the opportunity to gain *bonn*. (Recall how the Buddha accepted the tainted meal that was to lead to his death, not from misplaced politeness but in order to give the donor the chance to earn merit.) Contributing to the upkeep and beautification of monasteries also gains *bonn*, as does participation in *bonn*-producing festivals, such as Kathen, held at the end of the monsoon retreat in October or November, when robes and other gifts are offered to the monks.

*Bonn*-making is not restricted to the monasteries and the monkhood. The housewife who puts out offerings for the household gods gains *bonn*, as do those who honour their parents. Giving to beggars also earns *bonn*, but not so much as these other acts.

Vannak needs *bonn* in a hurry. He will gain it by going to the monks to be sprinkled

*Offerings at Preah Ang Doung Kar.*

with holy water and have red threads tied around his wrist. He will not, however, gain enough to overcome his inherent *kamm*, the *kamm* with which he was born, and which accounts for his present lowly status in life. He is, and will remain, a man of *kamm*.

## The Man of *Bonn*

Professors Trude Jacobsen and Martin Stuart Fox have published the results of a study of power and political culture in Cambodia, which I've relied on for what follows.

The man of *bonn* (a *neak bonn* or 'man of merit') is distinguished by outward signs, such as authority (*omneach*), power (*komlang*) and status (*bon sak*). His business interests span property, plantations, the tourism industry, the garment industry, import/export, banking and finance. All his projects are above board, yet also somewhat mysterious, for the man of *bonn* dislikes publicity. The mystery adds to the awe in which he's held. He will have government and/or royal titles (*okhna*, the most common, is the equivalent of a knighthood), live in a large house in a good suburb, and be seen around town in the latest-model cars (he'll own several, all kept up to date each year), accompanied by bodyguards. Do not touch the car of a man of *bonn*, do not scratch it, for the bodyguards are armed.

He will associate with others like himself, including appropriately high-status foreigners. He will play golf at the best clubs and be seen at expensive restaurants and upmarket nightspots. Two or three times a year, maybe more, he will visit Seoul and London, his wife will shop in Singapore and his children will study in Sydney and Paris. This is not indulgence. Without outward show no-one would recognise him for a man of *bonn* and he would risk losing all. With it, he is visibly a *neak thom* ('big man').

*Neak thom* possess *boramey*, the power of charismatic speech. This is not simple oratory, although the man who possesses *boramey* will be a good orator, but the more subtle power of speech that compels attention. Sihanouk had *boramey*, Pol Pot had it and Hun Sen has it. Paradoxically, the man who possesses *boramey* will be silent at gatherings, power being more awesome when not exercised, but when he speaks all others fall silent. The speech of the *neak thom* is magical.

He will be at the centre of a network of *khsae*, the 'strings' of client-patron relationships that provide the framework for Cambodian life. As a patron he will be the protector and benefactor of those below him, providing favours through his power and influence. These favours might include finding a job for a client's son, helping with legal or personal problems involving his own or other *khsae*, influencing business deals on his behalf or arranging an advantageous marriage – in short all those things that enable society to run smoothly. In return the client will support the patron according to his own ability and his patron's needs.

In the absence of a neutral framework for social interaction, all relationships must be personalized. The patron is not only a *neak thom*, he is also a *bong thom*, a big brother, and he cares for his clients as if they were members of his own family. One can no more change one's patron than one can change one's parents. Yet if a great man shows signs of weakness, if his power and status falter, his clients will desert him. Even the highest in the land can never rest but must always look to their positions if they wish to remain *neak thom*.

Most men will be simultaneously client and patron. Ta Krit, the retired headman of Prek Luong village, was the patron of Hang Sovann the village artist, and would have his own patrons in the district, who would have had theirs in the capital, all of which would account for Ta Krit retaining his position for 30 years. The traffic cop who sits at the intersection in Phnom Penh extracting on-the-spot fines will share the proceeds with his captain, who will share with the colonel, and the millionaire contractor who constructs the highway that foreign donors pay for will share a cut with the officials who put the contract his way. Westerners will see this as corruption, but while corruption is theft, *bonn* is merit.

Merit comes from wisdom and wisdom from *dhammapul*, which is nature, and so the force that binds client and patron is as morally neutral as the law of gravity.

*Dhammapul* decrees that the man of *bonn* is born to greatness, but some great men are born in humble circumstances. That they have achieved greatness demonstrates that they possess much *bonn* from previous lives. Even former King Sihanouk, born into royalty but by no means the obvious candidate for the crown, owed his ascension to being the reincarnation of the illustrious Jayavarman VII, the builder of Angkor and architect of the Khmer empire.

The lives of the very highest *neak thom* are marked by signs. A fortune-teller predicted that a great leader of the Khmer people would come from Dey Leou village in Kampong Cham province. In 1952 a child was born to a peasant family in that village. The boy was Hun Sen, Prime Minister of Cambodia, but it was only in retrospect that people began to connect him to the prophecy.

The gods protect the man of *bonn*. Prior to a visit to Siem Reap in 1998, Hun Sen's brother-in-law had a dream in which he was told that Hun Sen did not pay enough attention to a divinity called Preah Ang Khmau ('Sacred Black Lord'). Hun Sen had never heard of this god, but he made inquiries and learned that Preah Ang Khmau was well known in Siem Reap, where he has a shrine. As soon as he arrived in Siem Reap, Hun Sen went to the shrine and paid his respects, and the god gave him an oracle: a king condemned a man to death but the man did not die, and it was well, for the man became a man of power. Next day would-be assassins fired four rockets at Hun Sen's car, but Hun Sen was unharmed, for Preah Ang Khmau had protected him.

## The Man of *Bonn's* Tale

On the afternoon of 3 March 2013 Keam Piseth Narita, a 23-year-old medical student, was driving her little brother and sister home from school when she hit a motorbike near the traffic circle at Independence Monument.

Being young and inexperienced, and quite possibly acting on her father's remembered advice about what to do in such a situation, she hit the accelerator and sped down Norodom Boulevard with the police in hot pursuit. After a chase lasting several kilometres she lost control of the vehicle outside the Ministry of the Interior, mowed down nine motorbikes and four bicycles, and smashed into a group of schoolchildren. Three were killed on the spot, 11 were seriously injured, and Piseth Narita was taken inside the Ministry to save her from lynching.

Speeding off from the scene of an accident is quite normal for Cambodia, as Ear Chariya, road safety programme manager at NGO Handicap International, explained to the *Phnom Penh Post*: "Drivers who are involved in a crash are afraid that if they stop, people will hit them or kill them … People think that justice won't occur, that the guilty party won't be punished, and there are many cases where justice doesn't occur."

The accident happened on a Friday. On the following Monday, Piseth Narita's mother and father joined a huge procession led by a hundred monks down Norodom Boulevard from the Monument to the scene of the crash. There they wept with the parents of the lost children, begged for forgiveness and offered compensation for their daughter's act.

Some of the parents were willing to forgive, but others were not. "I can understand the feeling of the suspect's parents who have come to my son's funeral and asked for forgiveness," said the mother of a dead eight-year-old, "but I won't sell my child's life. I want to see this driver in jail more than I want compensation. He was my only son and now he is gone."

Three months later, on 12 June, Piseth Narita appeared in court. She was fined 6,000,000 riel ($1,500) for dangerous driving and sentenced to three years in prison, the maximum fine and sentence available under the law. She had already served three months and the judge, noting extenuating circumstances (the accused, he said, had been taking medication that made her drowsy behind the wheel), suspended the remainder. Piseth Narita had served one month for each life taken. All the families had by now accepted compensation, rumoured to be $20,000 each, and withdrawn their complaints. There would be no civil cases.

Ou Virak, president of the Cambodian Center for Human Rights, told the *Phnom Penh Post* he felt the judge had been far too lenient, but the executive director of the Community Legal Education Center, Yeng Virak (no relation – the first is Mr Ou and the second is Mr Yeng, and they share Virak as a personal name), pointed out that Piseth Narita had acted without intention to cause harm. She had also been given the maximum possible sentence. Indeed, he said, the fact that she was tried and sentenced at all was something unusual. "To me, it's quite, quite fair. If she commits the same thing in the future, she should be severely sentenced."

Piseth Narita was the daughter of the deputy director of Kandal Provincial Hospital. Her father was a man of *bonn*, although not the very biggest of *neak thom*, and what Mr Yeng was saying was that there had not been, as one might have thought (and as many said), any corruption of the process of law, for the man of *bonn* respects the gods, and the gods protect him and his.

✿

I've mentioned Piseth Narita's tale at length because it was a national *cause célèbre*, but also because it was somewhat unusual. Piseth was cornered inside the Interior Ministry with a mob at the gates and reporters on the scene, and there was no way she could escape arrest. The degree of public attention meant that the case had to go forward and could not simply be dropped. Cambodia is lawless, but not entirely so, and public opinion counts, especially in the capital.

Contrast that case with another, this one involving a *neak thom* far more powerful than the deputy head of a provincial hospital.

A little before midnight on 3 August 2008 a black Cadillac Escalade, travelling down Sothearos Boulevard at speed, smashed into a motorbike in front of the Regent Park Hotel. The driver of the motorbike, a crane operator named Sam Sabo, was dismembered. The driver of the Escalade, like Piseth Narita, tried to drive off, but he had shredded his tyres on the motorbike and had to stop not far away outside the Ministry of Justice. (The gods have a sense of humour.)

"Numerous traffic police were seen avoiding the accident scene," reported the *Phnom Penh Post*. The driver remained in the vehicle and on the phone, and within minutes two dozen armed military police arrived to secure the perimeter and remove his number plates. A witness told the *Post*'s reporter, "I heard the police tell the car driver, 'Don't worry, it wasn't your mistake it was the motorbike driver's mistake'." The reporter, who seems to have been quite fearless, interviewed one of the military police. The policeman told him, "It is very difficult and complicated because this accident involved a big person.

They will hide the story."

The big person was Hun Chea, a nephew of Hun Sen.

As with Piseth Narita's case, the incident attracted much media attention, and the Deputy Municipal Police Commissioner said he would open a file. "According to the law, it must be sent to court." A few days later he was declining to comment, and Sam Sabo's family were reported to have accepted $4,000 compensation in exchange for not filing a complaint. Hun Chea could not be reached, but his younger brother told reporters that the case was resolved. "It's not right what Radio Free Asia broadcasted, saying that it was unintentional murder. It was not. It was a normal traffic accident in which the motorbike driver was very drunk. Please stop broadcasting about this case, or I will file a complaint."

## The Beggar's Tale

Penh is a beggar on the Penh Penh Riverside, but a beggar with a certain claim to fame, because when he was very young the Magnum photographer, Philip Jones Griffith, included his picture in a book about Agent Orange. The photo was taken in 2000, long after the Vietnam War ended, but Agent Orange lingers through generations.

Griffiths says Penh is 14 in the photo but he looks younger, gazing up at the camera with big eyes, a handsome and intelligent little boy with no future and no arms or legs, because Agent Orange causes mothers to give birth to monsters.

Penh was born in Takeo province on the Vietnamese border, and his parents brought him to the capital at an early age because there was no support for his condition there. There's very little in Phnom Penh either, but an NGO provides a wheelchair and he begs along the Riverside, taking cash between the stubs of his flippers and pushing it into a special pouch sewn into his shirt.

Some years after that photo I interviewed Penh for a magazine, and asked him if he could explain his deformities – I was looking for evidence, in the form of family memories, of American planes spraying the village with defoliant. What he told me was quite different:

"I don't know why I was born this way. I never did anything wrong, never harmed anyone. People in my village say I must have done something very wrong in my previous life, but I don't remember my previous life. I used to try to remember when I was little, but I never could. I don't think about it any more. I try to be good in this life, and I hope I can be reborn to a good body in my next."

# 5 Ancestral Voices

*The legends of Cambodia cover the whole sweep of cosmic history, from the primordial crocodile kings, who ruled the Earth at the beginning of time, to Sacred Cow and Sacred Gem, whose fate mirrored that of Cambodia itself.*

## Preah Torani

The goddess who appeared from the earth at the Buddha's bidding to sweep away Mara's host (see page 12) was called Dharani, which means 'earth' in Pali. In Cambodia she's called Neang Kongheng, Lady Princess, or more formally Preah Torani, 'Sacred Earth'.

Torani (her name is pronounced *tornee*) is usually depicted riding on the back of a crocodile. The crocodile has no part in the story of the Buddha's Enlightenment, but it features in a myth concerning the creation of the earth. This tells how, before there was any land, Krong Bali, the crocodile king, and his brother, Preah Phum Reachea, the Sacred Earth King, played in the primordial cosmic ocean, stirring up storms with their mighty tails. The churning produced a scum that hardened to form the earth, of which they were the owners and rulers.

When the first Buddha of that age appeared he found that all the earth belonged to the crocodile brothers. He therefore asked Krong Bali for as much dry land as he could cover in three steps. Krong Bali agreed, thinking the Buddha could cover little in three steps, but the Buddha covered the whole earth, confining the crocodiles to the underworld.

The crocodile king asked the Lord Buddha for a boon, and the Buddha from his compassion decreed that whenever people celebrate a festival, or disturb the earth with building or farming, they should first make an offering to Krong Bali. If this is not done the crocodile will thrash his tail, bringing chaos and disaster.

In the legend Krong Bali and his brother are referred to sometimes as crocodiles and sometimes as *nagas*, as if there's no distinction. Both are associated with Torani. The royal chronicles of Cambodia, which are trustworthy as records of belief if not of history, tell how the goddess once appeared as a serpent to a king leading his army to battle, slithering in front of him towards the enemy and portending victory.

Bare-breasted Torani's most striking feature is her long snake-like rope of hair, and throughout Southeast Asia hair is associated with sexuality. Unmarried Cambodian girls traditionally wore their hair long, while married women put it up in a bun. It's also associated with danger – children traditionally had their heads shaved except for a forelock, to protect them from demons. At weddings, snips of hair are taken from both bride and groom for the same reason, and monks and nuns shave their heads to signify their conquest of Mara's daughters. And yet hair is also holy – the freshly shaved hair of a novice is not allowed to touch the ground but must be collected on a cloth, and the Buddha's own head is always covered in thick curls.

Torani is not in the story of the Buddha's Enlightenment as known in China, Japan, Tibet or even Sri Lanka. Her popularity is strictly confined to mainland Southeast Asia, and she seems to have arrived between the 8th and 12th centuries from north-east India, where she has Hindu cousins.

Reformers have tried to banish her on the grounds that she's not in the official scriptures, but she can be found wringing out her hair everywhere. She decorates a fountain outside Phnom Penh's Olympic Stadium, she's to be found on funeral stupas and the pillars holding up *tevoda* shrines and she's ubiquitous in monasteries. She's at Prasat Banteay Thom at Angkor and at Wat Phnom she stands opposite Daun Penh in front of the Buddha. And like the *tevoda* she's female, marking Cambodia as a country where the feminine retains a powerful presence in the unseen world.

## Preah Thong and the *Naga* Princess

In India there once lived a prince, Preah Thong by name, who was told in a dream to take a ship and sail to a golden land in the east where he would establish a great kingdom. So the prince prepared his ship and crew and set forth, and after many days sailing came upon a beautiful and uninhabited island. Preah Thong named it Nokor Kok Tlok, Kingdom of the Tlok Tree, after a large tlok tree by the shore. Possibly feeling he had done enough for one day Preah Thong fell asleep under the tlok tree, and when he awoke it was night. The moon was full and he gazed on the sea, wondering about his new kingdom, and especially about the lack of people, and as he watched he saw human figures emerge from beneath the waves.

The prince watched from behind the tree as the beings spread a feast under the trees. The men fell to sport, wrestling and sword-playing on the sand, while the women strummed musical instruments and sang sweet songs. All were comely, but in their midst was a lady more beautiful than any. Overcome by her beauty, Preah Thong stepped out from his hiding place and introduced himself, asking the lady who she was, and how it came to be that she and her people lived beneath the waters.

The lady permitted him to know that she was Neang Neak (Lady Naga), the daughter of the *naga* king, that this was the land of the *nagas*, and that she and her court visited the beach every full moon night for their pleasure. She informed him also that it was a serious breach to speak to royalty before being spoken to, and that he had broken this rule, but as she could see he was a stranger and ignorant of *naga* etiquette, she would permit him to inform her of his name and family before ordering his execution.

Quickly Preah Thong told Neang Neak of his foreign origins and princely station and declared his love. After further gentle words the princess agreed to take him to the underwater kingdom of the *nagas* so that he could ask her father for her hand in marriage.

And so Neang Neak took Preah Thong to the kingdom of the *nagas*, the prince holding her scarf. For three days they celebrated their wedding, and at the end of that time the *naga* king swallowed the water that had covered the land and Preah Thong and Neang Neak ruled together over the Khmers.

In another version of the legend the Indian prince is a Brahmin named Kaundinya and the *naga* princess is named Soma. The plot is very similar to the story of Preah Thong and Neang Neak except that the island is apparently upstream in the Mekong, and Kaundinya defeats Soma in battle before she agrees to marry him. In yet another version the prince was called Kambu, from which comes the name Kambuja, Cambodia.

## The Tower of the *Naga* King

The great enemy of the Khmers were the Cham, whose kingdom of Champa lay along the central coast of present-day Vietnam. In the year 657 a Cham king named Prakasadhamma left an inscription in his capital telling how the Brahmin Kaundinya 'planted his spear' (settled) in Kambuja and took Soma, daughter of the *naga* king, as his wife. Prakasadhamma mentioned this because, although a Cham, he was a descendant of Kaundinya and Soma through his father, who was a Khmer prince.

The marriage of human prince and *naga* princess sounds fanciful, but the Chinese traveller Zhou Daguan says this in the record of his stay at Angkor shortly before the year 1300:

*Inside the palace there is a gold tower, at the summit of which the king sleeps at night. The local people all say that in the tower lives a nine-headed snake spirit which is the lord of the earth for the entire country. Every night it appears in the form of a woman, and the king first shares his bed with her and has sex with her. [...] If for a single night this spirit does not appear, the time has come for this [...] king to die.*

The tower is probably Phimeanakas, the only structure still remaining inside the palace compound. I climbed to the top one cloudy and tourist-free day in the monsoon season, but found no *naga*-maiden awaiting me. Given what happened to the mythical Leper King, husband to the *naga*-princess and son-in-law to the *naga*-king (see page 88), this may be just as well.

The myth is at least correct in that Brahmanic religion came to Cambodia from India. Nobody quite knows when or how this happened, although it seems certain there was no conquest or mass migration, and the process was probably in the hands of Southeast Asians exploiting the coastal trade route between India and China around the time when the Romans were building their empire.

At that time, before there were kingdoms, Cambodia was a land of villages ruled by clan and village chiefs who took their descent from the female line. If these ancestors were deified, as seems likely, the chiefs most probably claimed descent from female deities. The India/China trade allowed the chiefs to grow steadily wealthier, and as their chiefdoms grew into kingdoms they adopted Indian mythology and ritual to enhance their prestige. This is reflected in the Sanskrit titles they adopted – Indravarman, 'Protected by Indra', Suryavarman, 'Protected by Surya' (the sun), and all the other varmans so characteristic of Khmer kingship.

The first kingdoms had emerged by the time of Christ and probably a little earlier. Buddhism was present by at least the fifth and sixth centuries, when Khmer kings occasionally sent Buddhist monks to China on diplomatic missions, but it is unclear what school of Buddhism these monks belonged to, whether the Mahayana, followed today in China, Japan and Vietnam, or the Theravada, found in other parts of Southeast Asia and Sri Lanka.

By the ninth century a single large Khmer kingdom was established with its capital at or near Angkor. The dominant gods (gods supported by the kings) were Shiva and Vishnu, but Buddhism was at least tolerated. (The idea of tolerance should not be pushed too far: an inscription from a monastery dedicated to Vishnu warns that Buddhist monks have bad morals and are not welcome.)

From the tenth century onwards there is increasing evidence of royal support for Buddhism. King Jayavarman VII, who reigned c.1181–1218, was the most powerful of all of the kings of Angkor, and a Buddhist, although not of the Theravada. He defeated his enemies – notably the Cham – built temples and hospitals, and reached out to other Buddhist kings in Sri Lanka and Burma, thus unintentionally opening Cambodia to Theravada, the dominant school in those kingdoms. Zhou Daguan, who stayed in Angkor a century after Jayavarman, records Brahmin priests, followers of Siva, and Buddhist monks who seem to be followers of Theravada, as they wore yellow robes with the right shoulder bare. He also records that every village had a temple and a tower, which some take to mean a Theravada monastery.

Soon after Zhou Daguan's visit both Shaivism and Mahayana disappeared, and by the time the semi-legendary King Ponhea Yat, the last king of Angkor, moved the capital to Phnom Penh, Cambodia had become Theravada Buddhist.

## Sacred Cow and Sacred Gem

The period between the sack of Angkor by the Thais in 1431 and the arrival of the French in the mid-19th century is the Cambodian Dark Ages. The kings were largely ineffectual, the capital shifted between Phnom Penh, Lovek and Oudong, and the kingdom was nibbled away by Siam and Vietnam, losing provinces and population to both. The architecture, in contrast to the stone temples of Angkor, was largely perishable, the inscriptions have been comparatively little studied, and although palace and monastic chronicles exist, they are unreliable and filled with legends. Those legends, while a poor introduction to history, are nevertheless an instructive guide to the Cambodian soul.

Preah Koh and Preah Keo were twin brothers. While their mother was pregnant with them she developed a craving for green mango, but in trying to climb the mango tree she fell to her death. As she died the twins were born, but while one was human, the other was a calf. The villagers chased them into the forest, where Preah Koh, the Sacred Cow, fed and clothed his brother by belching up feasts from his belly. (In one version Preah Koh's belly contains sacred texts, implying the wisdom and knowledge inherited from the past.)

Preah Keo grew up to be a handsome young man. One day, clothed in a royal costume belched up for him by Preah Koh, he was loitering by a forest pool when the king's youngest daughter, Neang Pov ('Youngest Princess') came to bathe. Preah Keo drew near and spoke charmingly to the princess, and she, enchanted by the handsome young prince, allowed him to kiss her. When her father, the king, heard of this he was furious and had Neang Pov beheaded, but Preah Koh magically restored her head to her shoulders and belched out a palace from his magic belly, where Indra, the king of the gods, presided over her wedding to Preah Keo.

At this time the king of Siam was trying to conquer Cambodia. Unsuccessful in battle, he challenged the king of Cambodia to a cockfight, knowing there was no fighting cock in Cambodia that could hope to defeat the Thai fighting cock. The Khmer court were in despair, until Preah Koh took pity and changed himself into an invincible fighting cock, in which form he defeated the King of Siam's bird.

The furious Thai king challenged the Cambodians to a fight between elephants. Once again the Khmer were despondent, and once again Preah Koh saved them, transforming himself into an invincible fighting elephant.

The king of Siam consulted his astrologers: why was he always defeated by the Khmers, even though he was far more powerful? The astrologers consulted their charts and discovered the secret of Sacred Cow. The power of Preah Koh, they advised the king, could not be defeated by normal means nor even by magic, but if the king should construct a mechanical bull, the Khmer cow could be vanquished.

Once more the Thai king challenged the Khmers to a duel. When Preah Koh saw the mechanical bull he knew at once that he would be defeated, but he accepted the challenge. As he had foreseen, his magic blows had no effect on the Thai bull, which managed to knock off one of his magic horns. Deciding to escape and fight another day, Preah Koh called Preah Keo and Neang Pov to cling to him and flew off.

As they flew through the skies Neang Pov lost her grip and fell to her death, where Indra turned her into a sacred mountain, but the brothers flew on and landed at Lovek, the capital of their king. There they hid in a bamboo forest, thinking they would be safe, but the devious Thai loaded their cannons with silver coins and fired them into the forest, and the local villagers thoughtlessly cut down the bamboo to find the coins. Preah Koh and Preah Keo were captured and the king of Siam took them to his capital, where they remain to this day, imprisoned in a beautiful palace, weeping as they look eastward towards Cambodia.

The legend of Sacred Cow and Sacred Gem operates on many levels. At one, Sacred Cow is the modern descendant of the bull Nandi, the vehicle of the god Shiva, handed down and distorted through centuries of folklore. Preah Keo rides on his back with Neang Pov like Shiva riding on Nandi with his wife Parvati, goddess of the mountains, of love and of devotion.

At another level Preah Koh with his magic stomach and invincibility in battle represents the lost power of ancient Angkor, as well as, in his defeat and captivity, Cambodia's ultimate humiliation and powerlessness. Sacred Gem is a real gem, the Emerald Buddha, once held by Cambodia, at least according to Cambodian legend, and now the national icon of Thailand.

And finally, there's real history, or what might be real history. In the 15th century there was a king – a real one – named Ang Chan, who had his capital at Lovek. Ang Chan was a powerful king who kept the Siamese at bay, but in time the throne passed to his grandson Preah Prattha, who was weaker. The Siamese king, finding the Khmer too powerful to defeat in battle, consulted his astrologers and learned that Lovek was protected by a powerful four-faced Buddha statue. The city would never fall so long as this statue remained in the city. The Siamese king sent a fraudulent holy man to Lovek, who convinced Preah Prattha to give the Buddha to the Thais. And so Lovek was captured and Cambodia's greatness passed away, not because of the power of her enemies, but because of the weakness of the Cambodians themselves.

Visitors to the monastery of Wat Tralaeng Kaeng at Lovek can see the feet of the huge four-faced Buddha statue still in place – the statue itself is at the bottom of the river, not far away, having sunk the boat onto which the Siamese loaded it. Also to be seen is a statue of Sacred Cow and Sacred Gem under a bodhi tree growing round a mango tree. Sprouting from the tree is a single mango branch, which is all that remains of the tree from which their mother fell at their birth.

A little beyond the bodhi tree is the entrance to one of the underground passageways of the *nagas*, revealed when the *naga* king drank up the ocean and exposed Srok Khmer, the land of Cambodia, for his daughter and son-in-law. There are many such tunnels and caves around Cambodia, and this one extends from Lovek to Oudong, where the *naga's* tail brushes against the sacred funeral urns of the ancestors of the present king.

By the 19th century the king of Cambodia, now established at Oudong, was a vassal of his neighbours, sometimes the Vietnamese emperor and sometimes the Thai king. Even his coronation had to be conducted in Bangkok, because the Thais held the sacred royal regalia.

In the mid-19th century Rama IV of Siam began a reformation of Thai Buddhism, which he believed had been in decay since the Burmese destroyed the Thai capital Ayutthaya a century earlier. He had the scriptures translated into Thai (a major innovation

– they'd always been in Pali) and tightened the standards of monkish behaviour so that deportment, dress and all the other rules of the monkhood were strictly observed. The reform movement was called the Dhammayutika, 'those who uphold the Teachings', while those who remained unreformed were called the Mahanikaya, 'those who follow tradition'.

At this time it was the custom for Cambodian kings to send their sons to the Thai court to learn Thai ways, thus in 1850 King Ang Duong sent his 16-year-old son Norodom to Bangkok. Part of the prince's education was in religion, and Norodom's induction as a Dhammayutika novice was sponsored by King Mongkut himself.

In 1860 Ang Duong died, and Norodom, now 26, went back to Oudong to ascend the throne. Or he would have ascended it, except that Siam refused to release the royal regalia. Norodom arrived in Oudong without the status of kingship, and was soon chased out again by Cham rebels and Vietnamese invaders. He took refuge in Bangkok, and the king of Siam, not wishing to see Cambodia pass into Vietnamese hands, decided to crown him after all. The ceremony took place in Bangkok in 1863.

Norodom was now formally king, but he was still a Thai vassal. Between the Vietnamese on one side and the Thais on the other, it seemed Cambodia might soon vanish from the map. At this dire moment the French arrived.

They had already captured Saigon (present-day Ho Chih Minh City) in 1859, and in 1862 the Emperor of Vietnam had been forced to cede the south to them. The French were clearly powerful, and Norodom asked them to establish a protectorate over his kingdom. In 1867 the Thais were forced to give up all claim over Cambodia, receiving the three Western provinces of Battambang, Siem Reap and Banteay Meanchey in compensation (they were returned to Cambodian control in 1907), along with the royal regalia. In 1868 Norodom was crowned a second time, this time as the ruler of a kingdom under French protection and free from Thai and Vietnamese domination.

Norodom turned his mind to his country's spiritual welfare. One part of this was to reform Cambodian religion along Tommayut lines, as the Dhammayutika movement was called in Khmer. The Tommayut were and still are a tiny minority of the monkhood, but it is Tommayut monks who officiate at all royal ceremonies. Their disagreements with the majority Mahanikaya revolve around such details as whether monks should wear sandals on the alms round or go barefoot (the Tommayut say barefoot), how the begging bowl is to be carried and the pronunciation of the Pali scriptures.

All this underlines a crucial and significant distinction between religions: Christianity is a religion of belief (orthodoxy means correct belief), and Christians have murdered each other over such questions as whether the Son proceeds from the Father. Buddhism, by contrast, is a religion of orthopraxy, correct practice, and Buddhists largely don't care what other Buddhists believe so long as they follow correct conduct. A monk could conceivably hold that reincarnation is a mistaken belief and that merit-generating acts are a waste of time without attracting untoward comment, but in late 19th century Phnom Penh the monks were attacking each other in the street with clubs over the question of whether or not to go barefoot on the alms round.

# 6 The Ordination of the *Naga*

*What is a Buddhist monastery? What motivates a man to become a monk? What is the life like? Why do they shave their heads? Why do they beg? (The answer is that they don't.) A brief guide to the way of the robe.*

## The Monastery

A monastery is a wat, from a Pali word meaning an enclosure, and the wat is marked off from the world by a wall decorated with an eight-spoke wagon-wheel symbolizing the Eightfold Path and topped by small symbolic and magical boundary stones called *seila*. The monastery gates are decorated with symbols, usually related to Buddhism but occasionally whimsical – a monastery across the river from Phnom Penh, at a place called Prawn Lake, has gates flanked with giant prawns. In the villages the monastery gates are always open, but in the city they are locked at night.

The Buddha's birth, enlightenment and first sermon all took place in a garden, and the gods of Meru live amid gardens, so the wat is laid out as a garden, a place of shady paths and garden beds swept scrupulously clean every morning by the novices and temple boys. The garden will usually be decorated with a large bodhi tree, a collection of instructive statues, a shrine for the *neak ta*, tablets recording donations, and tables and benches for study and relaxation.

*Monastery shrine hall.*

The main building is the *preah vihear*, the prayer hall. Built on a raised platform and marked off from the rest of the monastery by a low wall, the *vihear* is easily recognized by its elaborate multi-tiered roof and tall spire. Usually there will be two or three tiers, but royal foundations will have more. The spire represents Meru, the home of the gods (see page 7).

Holding up the roof are the *garuda*-eagles who guard the lower slopes of Meru, sometimes accompanied by giants and the half-woman, half-bird figures called *kinori*. The flat gable ends are decorated with writhing *nagas*, and at the peak of each, where the tails of the two *naga* meet, is a decorative spike which is a stylized *garuda*. (Or so the written sources tell me, as well as my *kru* from the Ministry of Culture, but one Thai scholar, Promsak Jermsawatdi, suggests they might be derived from the horned masks found on the gable-ends of buildings in the Indonesian islands, part of the animistic belief system that underlies all Southeast Asia.)

Outside the *vihear* there will usually be a pair of spirit flags (*tung rolok*), which serve to alert the worshippers that a festival or other event is being held. The flag is a vertical banner with a triangular 'head', a rectangular 'body', two 'feet' at the bottom and triangular pennons off the main body. Bamboo rods are stuck through the body, the number indicating who the ceremony is for – father, mother, monks, the Buddha, the teaching, etc. I've been told the flags should always go behind the hall, never in front of it, but the ones I've seen are always in front. Socheat, my friend and interpreter, who told me this was the practice in his home village, was quite shocked to see how things were done in Phnom Penh.

Because the wat is a place for study and education there will also be a library and a hall for teaching the *dhamma*. Like the *vihear* these halls will have elaborate roofs, but not a spire.

Finally there are the functional buildings, including the monks' accommodation (*kot*) and the kitchens and ablution blocks, plus a collection of more or less ornate stupas or *chedey*, the shrines for the ashes of the dead, around the outer boundary wall.

The residents of the wat are, of course, the monks, but they also include *achar*, who are specialists in religious ritual. These two are the most respected classes of the monastic residents. Ranked below them in prestige are the *daun chi* – often but incorrectly called nuns – and the temple boys, who are orphans or boys from poor families placed in the wat by their parents, so that they can have the chance of an education, and students from the provinces too poor to afford a room in the city. At the bottom is a shifting population of beggars, drug addicts and petty criminals, and, at the very bottom, the monastery cats, who seem to be tolerated but not actively cared for. All, even the cats, gain their share of merit from living within the walls of the monastery.

Wat Preah Yu Vong is one of my favourite monasteries in Phnom Penh, not least because it's utterly atypical. The main gate is on Norodom Boulevard south of Independence Monument. The gate is never closed, and indeed can't be closed, because only the decorated arch remains. It gives on to what looks like, and is, a network of narrow residential alleys. I'm told the alleys are the unsafe haunt of drug addicts and petty criminals, but it looks peaceful enough at mid-morning, a time when evil-doers are still in bed.

Once upon a time Wat Preah Yu Vong was just like any other monastery, neither particularly famous nor particularly obscure, housing the normal number of monks in the normal complement of buildings. Everyone, monks, nuns, temple boys and cats, lived happily together until fall of Phnom Penh to the Khmer Rouge on 17 April 1975. The Khmer Rouge were the enemies of religion, and the monks of Wat Preah Yu Vong, like all others, were disrobed and sent to labour camps, where no doubt most of them died.

Phnom Penh fell again, this time to the Vietnamese and renegade ex-Khmer Rouge, on 7 January 1979, a date that continues to be celebrated as Victory Day. Traumatized Cambodians began making their way back to the city, searching for lost families and lost homes or simply for food. The first to arrive squatted in whatever houses they could find; if the true owners returned later they could either fight for their rights or just move on. Mostly they moved on. People began living in parks, along the river, and wherever else they could find a place and build a home from sheets of tin and plastic. One such place was the abandoned Wat Preah Yu Vong.

A former nun named Koma Pich made her home in the *preah vihear*. Koma Pich was the *chul rup* (a vehicle) for a *boramey*, or in other words, a shaman. She installed her gods (meaning their statues) in the *preah vihear* and offered help and advice to anyone in need, which in those days was practically everyone. Her performance as a shaman was electrifying, and so great was the respect in which Koma Pich was held, and so entrenched her position, that when monks returned to the wat they were unable to expel her. The *vihear* was simply divided in half, the monks on one side and Koma Pich on the other.

At first the government placed severe restrictions on the monks, not even allowing them to leave the monastery for the daily alms round, but time and the political tide were on their side. By the late 1980s religion was being viewed with official favour again, and the head monk asked the authorities to give back the temple. The authorities agreed, and Koma Pich packed her gods and vanished from history.

With the *vihear* back in their hands, the monks installed new Buddha images (the originals had disappeared, nobody knew when or where) and painted scenes from the life of the Buddha on the walls so that it became a proper temple again. But the grounds remained overrun with squatters. They'd subdivided the monastic buildings and built them into their houses, turned the garden paths into alleys, planted gardens and set up teashops, and so turned Preah Yu Vong into an urban village. Even the stupas had disappeared inside people's living rooms, ghosts or no ghosts. The monks tried to buy up the houses, but the price of real estate had started to rocket, the monks were poor, and nobody wanted to sell.

And that's where things remain today, a single ornate roof sheltering a handful of monks floating over a sea of quite solid little houses.

## The First Monk's Tale

Wat Preah Yu Vong now has just nine monks, a very small number for a monastery in Phnom Penh, and its history was told to me by one of them, Thach Panith. As his mixed Vietnamese-Khmer name indicates, he's Kampuchea Krom, meaning an ethnic Khmer from southern Vietnam, although his parents settled in Cambodia long ago. They placed him in a village monastery as a temple boy when he was very young because they couldn't afford to feed and educate him. He liked the monastic life and became a novice at the age of 15. Eventually he became a full monk, graduated from Buddhist high school, and moved to the capital and Wat Preah Yu Vong. He's now studying archaeology at the Royal University of Fine Arts. He enjoys the subject and wants to study more in order to use his knowledge to benefit society.

When he gets sick he prays to Preah Put (the Buddha) and to his dead parents. Belief in spirits and the ancestors, he says, predates Buddhism, and the people can't forget them. For this reason he doesn't criticize people who follow different religions or who believe in spirits. He can't say these people are bad or wrong, because he's met people who say they've seen the *mrieng kongveal* and the *chumneang pteah*, although he never has himself, and he thinks they spoke the truth for them. He enjoys the life of a monk, the prayer and study and meditation, and has no thought of leaving the monkhood.

Pralung Pheakdey ('Spirit of Honesty') is different. He's 23 and he's been a monk for six years. An orphan of sorts, he was brought up by his grandmother in a village in Kandal province and entered the monkhood both because he wanted to earn merit for his lost mother and because a *kru* told him that his mother would come back if he became a monk.

His mother disappeared when he was eight years old. He can't remember her, but people in the village have told him she might have gone to Thailand to look for work. He can't remember her face. His father divorced his mother about the time he was born. He knows his father but has never spoken to him and doesn't want to. His father, he says, was irresponsible, gave him life and then abandoned him. He's not certain if he will be a monk forever, because he doesn't like public speaking, and monks have to do a lot of public speaking, such as giving sermons.

## The Monkhood

The monk (*lok sangh*) has placed himself outside normal life, aiming at liberation from *samsara*, the cycle of birth and rebirth within the six spheres of existence.

Monks are not priests: one joins the monkhood to further one's own personal search for enlightenment, not to act as a mediator between God and man. The monk has superior access to the means of liberation, but not to the gods. Indeed, one of the first steps on the road to enlightenment is the recognition that gods and spirits don't exist except as illusions.

According to Cambodian tradition all boys should become novices for a limited period at a very young age. This is still the custom in the villages, but not so much in the city. Of those who go on to become full monks as adults, some do so for a short period before marriage or after a parent's funeral, or for one rainy season; some, especially

*Young monks in their saffron robes.*

from poor families, join in order to get an education; and some, of course, are religiously motivated, whether from advancing age or natural inclination.

The procedure for becoming a monk is designed to exclude persons of bad character. A candidate for the monkhood, as distinct from the novitiate, must be male, of good reputation, literate and over 20 years old. He (there are no nuns) begins by choosing a temple and expressing his wish to the head monk. Having been accepted, he must sign a form, witnessed by respected local laypersons, saying that he is of age and in good health, not in debt or guilty of any crime, and that his parents and wife, if he has these, have no objection to his decision.

Having done all this he can undertake the ordination ceremony. This is called 'the ordination of the *naga*', and the reason is as follows:

In the time of the Buddha's earthly life a *naga*, desiring to follow the Way, took human form and was ordained as a monk. He kept his human form all day, but that night, asleep in his *kot*, he returned to the form of a serpent, much to the horror of those who shared the room. The Lord Buddha summoned the *naga* and told him he could not remain as a monk, which is a privilege reserved for humans. At this the *naga* began to weep because his desire for enlightenment was great, and so the Compassionate One gave him the Five Precepts as the means to attaining a human existence in his next life. From that time all candidates for the monkhood, sincerely seeking enlightenment, are called *nagas*. In traditional rites the spirit of a *naga* was asked to take up residence in the new novice, but modern reformers have tried to stamp this out as a Brahmanical belief.

The life of the monk is strictly disciplined. There are many rules to follow, and the list of offences, the oldest of all Buddhist documents, is recited once a fortnight in front of all the monks. Murder, theft, sexual intercourse and making false claims to supernatural powers or to great spiritual attainments are extremely serious and will result in immediate expulsion from the Sangha. The rest of the rules are a mix of lesser sexual offences and regulations for teaching laypersons, as well as miscellaneous restrictions covering diet, deportment and almost every aspect of daily life.

The rules stipulate that the monk must eat only what he collects on the morning alms round, and must not eat after midday. The emphasis in alms-giving is not on what is given, but how it is given and received, respectfully and mindfully on both sides. In theory the alms should be food, but in practice it is often cash. This creates a problem, as a monk should not handle money, and for this reason the monk never touches the money.

The monk should not have any worldly possessions beyond a very short list of basics: razor, needle and thread, and a few other items. But Buddhism is flexible, and the modern monk can possess a pen, a mobile phone and other modern essentials.

Laypeople frequently wish to donate expensive gifts, such as plasma TVs, cars and refrigerators, to monks they respect, although in theory these should form the common property of the monastery.

The exterior signs of the monk are his saffron robe and shaved head and eyebrows, shaved first at ordination and then every month thereafter. (In keeping with the emphasis on praxis rather than belief, Thai and Cambodian monks visiting Burma are shocked to discover that Burmese monks do not shave their eyebrows.) A monk is expected to be dignified, calm and self-controlled. Mindfulness (self-control) is highly valued, and a monk's popular respect will often depend more on his deportment than on his learning or the quality of his preaching.

Monks must be treated with respect. Laypersons should always make sure that their heads are lower than the heads of monks, and should always uncover their heads in the presence of a monk or while inside the grounds of the monastery. There is a special language for addressing monks. Women, as the greatest obstacle to the monk's attainment of his goals, must be especially careful to avoid all physical contact with them: a woman should never pass a book or glass of water directly to a monk, even if he is her own younger brother, and a monk and a woman should never be alone together. Needless to say, monks should never eat in public places, such as cafes, or attend karaoke, or otherwise lower the prestige of the robe, and young novices should not play games or be loud and boisterous, but always quiet and dignified.

In theory, the life of the monk is one of study and meditation. In practice, study takes precedence over meditation, and the study of secular subjects (computer science, English, etc) over the holy texts.

Nevertheless, a monk will receive a thorough education in religion. He will attend Buddhist schools and universities, and sit for examinations in subjects, such as the lives and teachings of the Buddha and the rules of monastic conduct. As he advances the study and the examinations become harder, and the range of subjects broadens. Success in exams leads to prized titles, and these will add to the ex-monk's prestige and employability should he later return to lay life.

Any individual who enters the monkhood will gain merit, no matter what his motivation, and the merit will stay with him even if he leaves. There is therefore no stigma attached to leaving the monkhood.

In theory the monk withdraws from the world in order to follow the path to personal enlightenment; in practice he remains fully part of the community, although a very special part. He makes the daily alms round, and with other monks he attends weddings and funerals and merit-making ceremonies such as ordinations and precept-days, where he recites chants that he learned by heart in his earliest days in the robe. He might become famous for his sermons or his ability with amulets and holy water, in which case he can gain a personal following who will seek his guidance on matters from family life to medical problems. Many monks devote themselves to a life of study and meditation as the Buddha intended, and a few become hermits. Some, especially younger ones in the cities, are active in social issues and in protesting against injustice. Many are poor and are looking for an education. Very few are looking for an easy life.

## Study and Meditation

The aim of the monk's life is to grasp the reality of the illusory world through study and meditation, and the practice of virtue. His study is in Pali, which is to Theravada as Latin was to the medieval Church. As in the Church, there is a canon of holy books: some books are in it, while others, even though written in Pali, are not.

The canon is called the Tipitaka in Pali, meaning 'Three Baskets', because it's in three divisions. The three are the Vinaya, the rules and customs of the monkhood and the often-entertaining stories of their origins; the Sutta, the sermons of the Buddha and his closest followers; and the Abhidhamma, which concerns metaphysics and the study of mental processes. They add up to a collection thicker than a bible. The Three Baskets are accompanied by thick commentaries, also in Pali, compiled in Sri Lanka in the period between the third and fifth centuries of the modern era. All in all the Tipitaka and the commentaries make up a vast body of learning for the monk to master. To assist him, Cambodia has a network of Buddhist primary schools, high schools and universities. These follow the same curriculum as secular schools but add studies in Pali, Sanskrit and the Tipitaka.

Monks can find assistance to study overseas through sponsorship and scholarship programmes, often funded through foreign donors. Between 1993 and 2008 about 300 monks gained scholarships to study at universities in India, Sri Lanka, Myanmar and Japan. Monks make excellent students, or so the Buddhist authorities say, but the emphasis is on rote learning.

The aim of the monastic life is release from the cycle of rebirth and the attainment of nirvana. Nothing can be said about nirvana except that cause and effect end and the ultimate nature of reality manifests itself, or becomes manifest to itself – the language becomes extremely abstruse, as well it might when attempting to describe the indescribable. It is because nirvana is indescribable that monks supplement study with meditation.

Meditation has three distinct but interconnected purposes:

• To calm the mind, by withdrawing from the endless stream of sense impressions that make up ordinary reality, and to which the mind bears the same relationship as a leaf floating on a rushing stream.

• To concentrate the mind, shifting the attention from the stream (the world of sense-impressions) to the leaf itself (the mind).

• To lift the leaf out of the stream so that it can experience 'things as they are'.

There are many types of meditation, but the most common is *vipassana*, or insight meditation.

*Vipassana* was developed in Burma in the 19th century from a far earlier tradition and spread rapidly from the 1950s onwards. A large part of its popularity must be put down to its comparative ease (compared, that is, to more traditional meditation techniques – *vipassana* is far from easy for the beginner), and its promise of rapid results.

Being no expert on, or even amateur of, *vipassana*, I rely on *Instructions on Vipassana Meditation* by Venerable U Silananda, a Burmese master with an illustrious career in teaching Abhidhamma. Among other things, Sayadaw (teacher) U Silananda was one of the editors of the complete edition of the Tipitaka and its commentaries published following the Sixth International Buddhist Council – something like being a consultant for the King James Bible.

The mind in its normal state is like a cage of monkeys, gibbering and leaping, and unable to sit still. *Vipassana* teaches the student to sit still in the present moment, aware only of that moment. The student chooses an object on which to fasten the conscious mind – traditionally, the process of breathing – and concentrates on the six senses (sic), watching, observing and noting. The six senses are the usual five, plus the mind. This is most important, as the first aim is to control the mind. If the mind wanders, the student consciously observes the process of wandering, then returns it to the home object, the breath. In this way the mind ceases to be a cage of monkeys.

What happens when the mind ceases to be a cage of monkeys is beyond description. U Silananda does not attempt to describe it, not, at least, in this brief booklet given to visitors to the meditation centre at Phnom Penh's Wat Lanka. He warns that *vipassana* is not easy, and that it requires perseverance, patience and a teacher. He concludes by saying that whatever is gained through insight is not to be kept selfishly, but must be shared with others. Yet in the end each seeker after enlightenment must continue on his own path, at his own speed. U Silananda concludes with the Buddha's final words to his followers on the day of his nirvana: "Work out your salvation with diligence!"

# 7 Tales from the Monastery

*Who lives in the monastery? A chapter about achars, nuns, temple boys ... and monks.*

## The Second Monk's Tale

Wat Koh on Monivong Boulevard is one of the oldest monasteries in Phnom Penh. Founded by King Ponhea Yat in the early 15th century, it was destroyed in the 1970s and rebuilt in the 1990s. Its claim to fame is that the abbot has made it a refuge for stray and abandoned house pets. This is entirely in accordance with the Buddha's teaching of compassion for all living creatures, but I know of no other monastery that does it. Wat Koh has an even more notable eccentricity: the monks are forbidden to go out on the alms rounds in the morning, and the laypeople have to come to them instead.

Reach Kim Sam is a monk at Wat Koh and a graduate of Buddhist High School, which means that he is proficient in both Pali, which he began learning in Buddhist primary school, and Sanskrit. His studies covered both grammar and scripture and took up five hours a day, two in the morning and three in the afternoon.

*Vipassana* (see page 67), he says, is not meditation, as it is carried out under the guidance of a teacher; true meditation is done in solitude to calm the mind and reflect on what has been done during the day, and to discover whether one's actions have been positive or negative.

The aim of the monastic life is to escape *dukkha* (see page 22). Every human experiences *dukkha* because in life we meet problems, and these are *dukkha*. Sickness is *dukkha*, old age is *dukkha*, bereavement is *dukkha*, death is *dukkha*. Even those things we think are not *dukkha*, contain suffering. A couple who marry and have children will have happiness, but they will also have unhappiness, because every act contains *dukkha* in some measure. This was the beginning of the Buddha's insight into the nature of reality.

Yet despite this we should not refrain from action. Consider the man who sees a child in trouble in the river. The child calls out for help. The man can swim and could save the child, even though he knows that doing so will lead to *dukkha*. Can the man do nothing? No, because doing nothing is also action. He must save the child, because not to do so would be a lack of humanity. Perhaps the child has rescued the man in a previous life, so rescuing the child will be a return of merit for the one who once saved his life.

People are born with the *kamm* (negative energy) they have accumulated over the sum of their previous lives. *Bap* is what they add to it in this life. If a thief steals and is arrested, that is *bap*. If the thief is not arrested it is because he has accumulated *bonn* (merit) in previous lives, but eventually, if he continues to do evil, his *bap* will come to outweigh his *bonn*.

*A monastery cat at Wat Daun Penh.*

A monk is not selfish. He is motivated by compassion, just as was the Buddha. This compassion is exercised primarily on behalf of humans, but not solely, for animals are also living beings. The abbot's concern for animals comes from his understanding of the Buddha's teachings regarding compassion.

It was the abbot who decided that the monks of Wat Koh should not go out into the streets in the mornings to gather alms. He did this because many monks in the city collect alms at places where monks should not be seen, such as markets and beer-gardens, and even massage parlours. In crowded residential streets they enter apartment buildings where women dry their underwear, and at restaurants they stand outside in a manner that approaches moral blackmail. For this reason the abbot decided that laypeople who wish to support the monks of Wat Koh should bring their donations to the monastery, alowing them to gain merit while protecting the morality of the monks and the reputation of the Sangha.

## The Achar's Tale

An *achar* is a layperson who is an expert in ritual. Every monastery has at least two, one specializing in funerals and the other in weddings. Large monasteries will have several. They were almost all killed under the Khmer Rouge, documents were lost and knowledge was not passed on, but in recent years the Ministry of Religion has put a great deal of effort into training *achars*, including the creation of a Department of Research and Promotion of Buddhism and Connection to Society within the Ministry of Religion.

The chief *achar*'s position in a monastery can be difficult since, in addition to overseeing ritual and ceremony, he is in charge of the monastery funds. (He has to be – the rules of the Sangha forbid monks from touching money.) Since abbots tend to be strong-willed individuals, and since the funds are managed by a committee that includes laypeople, conflict is always in the air. So a good *achar* has to be an administrator, accountant and even a diplomat as well as an expert in ritual.

Net Sokun, aged 72, is originally from Prey Veng Province. He became a monk at the age of 12 at Nyroth Rangsey Monastery in Kdey Takoy village in Kandal Province, remaining there for 11 years before giving up the robe to work in the Ministry of Public Work and Transport and later at the Phnom Penh railway station. In 1975 he was forced to leave Phnom Penh by Pol Pot but he was re-employed after 1979 when a close colleague discovered he was still alive. A few years after this he married. He had nine children, but only seven are still living.

He continued to follow the Five Precepts after he left the monkhood. He always respected and followed the Buddha believing him to be the best and biggest teacher, for human beings, for gods, for *asura*, for ghosts and hell-beings, and for animals. The Buddha taught us the life cycle of birth, sickness and death. We were born with nothing and death brings us nothing, so we have to do good things for others while we are alive. The Buddha even sacrificed his life for others. (Sokun is referring to a story of the Buddha in a previous incarnation as a rabbit. He was, naturally, the most perfect of rabbits, but the god Shiva decided to test him and appeared in the form of an old man begging for food. The Buddha-rabbit built a fire, shook himself to get rid of fleas, and leapt into the fire to cook himself for his guest. Shiva placed him in the moon as a reminder of selflessness, and the moon-viewing festival, which is held on the night of the last day of the Water Festival, commemorates his sacrifice.)

Sokun retired from government service in 1998 at the age of 55 but continued working in the construction industry. He decided to surrender himself to the Buddha in 2010 in order to focus on the spiritual life. He stopped thinking about what he might like to eat, or saving money for anything or for anyone. He gave up all passions in everyday life, as he knew his life's journey could end at any moment. Since that time he has concentrated on building up merit by doing good deeds to prepare for a better life in the next incarnation, or to ascend to nirvana.

When he became an *achar* he attended a one-week training course, which involved 46 hours of instruction in 29 subjects, taught by experts and scholars from the Ministry of Religion, the Ministry of Art and Culture and the Ministry of Information; the course is wide-ranging and can include, for example, a lecture on traditional music delivered by a famous musician attached to the Royal Palace.

The aim of the course is that all *achars* throughout the kingdom should perform ceremonies in a uniform manner. This aim is further enforced by the guidebooks to various ceremonies. The official guide to weddings, for example, contains information about all aspects of the ceremony, from the correct way to carry out the hair-cutting ritual and the handling of flowers to the appropriate chants for the monks. Notwithstanding this, the guidelines are not meant to be rigid, and there is room for flexibility.

Most of the trainees are former monks. In fact it is extremely rare for someone who hasn't been a monk to become an *achar*, as the *achar* needs to know Pali and to be familiar with all kinds of texts and chants. In the past *achars* were always male, but the Ministry is making a conscious effort to train female *achars* and to reach out to *daun chi*, who have a great interest in religion but only haphazard means of gaining knowledge. The training course is very popular among both *achars* and *daun chi*, but the Ministry lacks adequate resources and places are limited.

People need to know that if they have plenty of *bonn* they will live longer, die a good death and rest in the Peaceful World. They will not be reborn from the Peaceful World. People experience rebirth only if they have a lot of unresolved *kamm* from bad deeds, which they must pay for. These unfortunate people are then reborn without legs, arms and eyes, or even as animals.

Going to the temple is like a learning process to reach a good destination, while going to live in a monastery is a good preparation for death. (I'm not sure what Sokun meant here – perhaps the 'learning process' refers to laypeople attending ceremonies at the temple, and the preparation for death applies to anyone who decides to live within a monastery.)

People believe that inviting a funeral *achar* to a wedding will bring bad luck to the new couple, or even lead to a death, but, in fact, a trained *achar* can lead any type of ceremony, because he has learned all the necessary rules and protocols.

Weddings and funerals are the main ceremonies he will attend, but *achars* are also expected to officiate at such rituals as a child's name-giving ceremony, the consecration of a new monastery, the exorcism of ghosts and the 'opening of the eyes' of a new Buddha image.

## The First Nun's Tale

Women who wish to follow the Way face a major obstacle: there are no nuns in Theravada Buddhism. I've called them nuns for convenience, but ordination in Theravada has to be part of a chain stretching back to the Buddha, and the chain for nuns died out long ago. Women may, however, become helpers to the monks and follow the eight precepts rather than the ten. These women are called *yeay chi* or *daun chi – yeay* and *daun* are both terms of respect for an older woman, with *daun chi* being the more formal.

Daun Chi Chan Sopheap started living in Wat Phnom Orderk ('Turtle Mountain Monastery') in Battambang province when she was not yet 20 years old. This was in the time of Lon Nol, who overthrew King Sihanouk in 1970. Not many years later the Khmer Rouge took control and sent her to a labour camp. After the Khmer Rouge were driven out she returned to the monastery in Battambang and lived there until she met the man who was to become her husband, a former monk who had been forced out of the Sangha by Lon Nol. (Lon Nol, concerned that too many potential soldiers were escaping conscription by putting on the robe, had decreed that no one under 50 could be a monk.)

For the next 25 years Sopheap lived with her husband and children in Battambang and later in Siem Reap. Around 2006 or 2007 she became very ill, and her husband agreed that she should return to Wat Phnom Orderk, where their second son was a

*Chan Sopheap, the first nun.*

monk. "By serving the monks as a *yeay chi* I would build up *kamma* to overcome my illness," said Sopheap, using the word in the correct Buddhist sense rather than the sense in which Vannak used the term *kamm*.

So she went back to Turtle Mountain, serving the monks and studying the Way, until her daughter asked if she would come with her to Phnom Penh where she wanted to do a ten-month course at the National Institute of Education. Naturally she agreed, as she could not send the girl to the city alone. She originally intended to take a room for the ten months, but rents in the capital proved too expensive and so, with the help of the abbot of Turtle Mountain, she obtained permission from the abbot of Wat Lanka to stay in this, one of the most prestigious monasteries in the capital.

I asked Sopheap about the spirits, as I was curious to know what an intelligent and learned woman would have to say about the spirit world.

"*Boramey* and *neak ta* are not part of Buddhism (*preah put sassana*). These things don't exist. Spirits come from Brahmanism (*prumman sassana*), which is all about the unseen. Brahmanism is about magic. I know of some people who came and asked a monk to sprinkle them and their new motorbike with holy water for good luck. That same day they were killed in an accident on the way home. Who can believe this? No pure monk will do this thing with magic water. Buddhism is about good and bad deeds. Your lot in this life reflects your deeds in your previous life. Everything that happens to you is due to the *kamma* that you've built up in your previous life and this one."

Sopheap will return to Battambang when her daughter's course is finished. The daughter will probably stay on in Phnom Penh as a teacher, and after a few years will apply for a scholarship to study for a Masters degree in English in Australia.

## The Temple Boy's Tale

Temple boys occupy one of the lowest rungs on the social ladder, but they can rise to great heights. Hun Sen's family were very poor, and when he was 13 he was sent to Phnom Penh to become a temple boy at Wat Neakavoan. Today, as everyone knows, he's the Prime Minister.

Souleang Keosupha is originally from a village in Ratanakiri province. He's 21 years old and in the first year of a law degree at Build Bright University. He has two brothers and a sister and is the third in his family. His father is a farmer but his mother passed away in 1997 following the delivery of his youngest sister. The baby survived, but the neighbours were convinced the mother's death was because an *arp* had eaten the placenta after they failed to bury it correctly.

Keosupha was 7 years old at the time and in the second grade. A monk from his village noticed Keosupha studying hard, and took pity on him because he was motherless and his family was extremely poor. Four years later the monk took Keosupha to stay with him at Wat Ounalom in Phnom Penh, where he was registered in Grade 2 at Preah Norodom Primary School, a kilometre from the monastery.

"Unlike other kids who cried when they were away from their family, I did not indulge in self pity but determined to return home a success, with pride.

Every morning I was woken up at 4 a.m. by the monk, who sometimes punished me or sprayed water on me if it took me too long to get up. When you are 11 years old, you know how difficult it is. Later I needed the alarm clock to wake me up, but now it's a habit to get up early.

As soon as I got up I started to learn Pali straight away, then my public school homework. All the temple boys were the same. After that we would sweep, clean, water the plants, boil water, cook and prepare the breakfast, and serve it. We ate after the monks had eaten, then we took turns washing the dishes. Only then could we go to school.

After school, we prepared the food that the monks got from begging, then served them lunch and finally we ate. Then we were allowed to take a nap. Sometimes we were taught English by the monks during our spare time, then we prepared our own dinner, using the leftover food from lunchtime.

During the rainy season we all had to participate in chanting from 8.30 a.m. to 9.00 a.m. We also chanted every time before we had meals. This merit-making was expressing gratitude to the donors for what they gave us to eat.

The monk supported me with clothes and study materials, using money that people gave him. Sometimes he asked people directly to buy me things.

My father has remarried now and has another two children. I only visit once a year, at Khmer New Year.

I am now doing a degree in law. I could have chosen to study technical skills but while these would be useful to me personally, by studying law I will be able to assist my community as whole, as there are innumerable disputes and conflicts in our province, and the villagers there really need my support.

The monk isn't able to support me financially, so I pay my own university fees with support from my parents and relatives. Plus, I supplement this with a part-time job as an assistant to a cameraman, and I'm able to earn around $50 a month.

In the future, I want to be a civil servant in the Provincial Department in Ratanakiri Province. I want to work as a lawyer or in fields related to the law.

I will always remember the words of the monk who, despite having so little, helped me to pursue my education up to tertiary level. I owe the monk and my family so much. I have to go back and help my village."

# 8 Domestic Gods

*The domestic gods are the spirits who guard the house. To them belong the tevoda shrine on its pillar outside, the shrine to the guardian goddess at the main house pillar and the shrine to the children of the fields hanging from a nail in the wall.*

## The Tevoda

Outside every Cambodian home is an ornate concrete dollshouse on top of a pillar. This is the shrine of the *tevoda,* who were once the *devata* that decorate the walls of Angkor. (see page 21).

Among the countless *tevoda* serving the gods on Meru were the seven beautiful daughters of Kbal Mohaprom, the god who ensures that the seasons come and go in their proper order and that the monsoon rain is neither too much nor too little. Men gave offerings to Kbal Mohaprom in thanks for the seasons and the rain, but one day these offerings stopped. On making inquiries the god learned of a young man named Thamabal who was renowned for his cleverness – indeed, so clever was he that he could understand the language of the birds. All offerings were now being made to Thamabal.

The furious Kbal Mohaprom dared Thamabal to test his cleverness: he would set a riddle, and if Thamabal failed to find the answer within seven days he would lose his head. Conversely, if Thamabal solved the riddle, Kbal Mohaprom would strike off his own head.

Thamabal accepted the challenge, and Kbal Mohaprom asked him: "Where is happiness in the morning, where is it at midday, and where in the evening?"

For six days Thamabal pondered the question but could not find an answer. On the evening of the last day, wandering in despair in the forest, he overheard two eagles talking.

"Will we eat meat tomorrow?" asked one.

"We will eat the clever Thamabal," said the other. "He can't find the answer to the riddle, and he will lose his head."

"Do you know the answer?" asked the first.

"Certainly! This is a riddle about where the Cambodian people find happiness. In the morning they wash the face so that happiness is cool water in the face, at midday they wash the body and happiness is in the body, and in the evening they wash their feet before they sleep. That is the answer."

And so when Thamabal appeared next morning before Kbal Mohaprom he was able to answer the riddle. Kbal Mohaprom was exceedingly angry, but being a god of his word he took his magic sword and cut off his head.

But the head of Kbal Mohaprom was not like any ordinary head, because it was made of fire. If it fell on the land it would burn up the land, if it fell into the ocean it would dry the sea and if it remained in the air it would drive the clouds away. Therefore, to save the world from destruction, the seven daughters of Kbal Mohaprom placed their father's head on a gold platter in a temple on Mount Kailash, the home of Lord Shiva. Each year, accompanied by all the tens of thousands of *tevoda*, they take it in procession around Meru, then bring it down to the world to see if men still retain sufficient merit to warrant saving.

The seven *tevoda* daughters of Kbal Mohaprom take it in turns to usher in Bon Chaul Chnam Thmey, 'Festival for Entering the New Year'. This falls at the end of the harvest season, usually the 13th or 14th of April according to the Western calendar.

At Wat Phnom a drummer begins beating the ceremonial tom-tom outside the *preah vihear* at exactly 7.45 a.m., a time set by the court astrologers as marking the departure of Tungsa Tevi, the *tevoda* of the old year. At 8:07 her sister and replacement Koraka Tevi arrive, seated on a tiger led by a horse (marking the fact that this was a Year of the Horse) and grasping a sword in her right hand and a cane in her left.

The arrival of Koraka Tevi was, unfortunately, invisible to all except the royal astrologers, but a group of formally dressed local Phnom Penh citizens and officials had gathered to welcome her. The astrologers announced over loudspeakers that the goddess brought blessings of rain for the farmers and peace and prosperity for the people. The worshippers the entered the shrine hall to make offerings of fruit, jasmine and lotus flowers before stepping outside again to distribute alms to the poor. Similar scenes are played out all over the city and the country.

Farmers are the ones most concerned by the message of the *tevoda*, and for them Koraka Tevi brought mixed news. On the positive side the coming year would see neither drought nor floods, but there would be some danger of damage to crops from outbreaks of insect pests, and rice prices would be low. Since the vast majority of Cambodians live in villages and depend on their own crops, this was a matter of no small importance.

For city people Khmer New Year is a time to return to their villages for the three days, and visitors who wish to experience the festival should also travel to a village. In Thailand the entire New Year festival is called Songkran and is a chance to get very wet, but water-throwing is banned in Cambodia, at least in the bigger towns.

The first day is called Maha Songkran and is devoted to the heavenly realm. People clean their houses and welcome the *tevoda* at her shrine. In the afternoon they visit the temple to pay respects and begin building a stupa out of sand next to the *preah vihear*. Teams of boys and girls play traditional games, which are a chance to flirt.

The second day is called Virak Wanabot and is devoted to the human world. People make offerings to their parents and donations to the poor. In the evening they go to the temple to pray to the ancestors and seek blessings from the monks.

The third day is called Leung Sak. On this day the Buddha, the monks, the ancestors and the elders are all honoured, and apologies are made for any mistakes made during the previous year. The monks are invited to complete the building of the sand-stupa, the Buddha statues are washed with perfumed water and children wash their parents' feet.

The *tevoda* shrine has little role to play in household life after the three days of New Year, but incense is burnt there throughout the year so that she will give blessings and protect the house and its inhabitants from the ghosts and demons that populate the human world.

## The First Shrine Merchant's Tale

Leng Sophoan runs a *tevoda* shrine workshop on Norodom Boulevard. About ten years ago she was in the cigarette business, but she saw an opportunity in shrines and got in just as the Phnom Penh property market took off. Booming house sales meant booming shrine sales, and from being a struggling cigarette merchant she now employs five workers and has been able to buy several houses as investments.

The shrines on display are priced from 30 to 40 dollars ("suitable for poor people") up to $2,000, with custom-designed models for extremely wealthy clients available for $20–30,000. Her buyers are both Khmer and Chinese. In the past her best periods were at Khmer and Chinese New Years, but now there are steady sales throughout the year. One of her sons, who is also in the shrine business and doing really well, makes up to a thousand dollars a day.

People buy shrines because they believe the *tevoda* will bring prosperity and grant their wishes. "The rich believe the most, and so they become richer, and the poor become poorer because they fail to believe."

The shrine-buyer takes on full responsibility for proper worship. The most important time is Khmer New Year, when offerings of lotus flowers should be made, and the shrine cleaned and decorated on the day before New Year begins. Incense should be burnt continuously for the three days, because the gods of Tavatimsa are pleased by sweet scents, as well as by pleasant music and graceful acts. Apart from at New Year, on holy days and at special festivals like Pchum Ben ('ancestors' day', a 15-day festival culminating in a national holiday when deceased relatives are commemorated, see chapter 11), the *tevoda* has to be offered flowers, food and drink appropriate to her tastes. (Koraka Tevi's favoured beverage is cooking oil, which leads to a spike in oil prices at New Year when it's her turn to visit Earth.)

Leng Sophoan's shrines come in two types: one like a dollshouse with the spired roof for the *tevoda* and a second type with a gabled roof without a spire for Preah Phum, 'Sacred Earth'. Leng Sophoan advises the would-be shrine owner to buy both types if possible, but if their budget doesn't stretch to two then the *tevoda* is preferable.

Rean tevoda (tevoda *shrine*).

Some years ago the Ministry of Culture became concerned that shrines were being made in many shapes and forms, reflecting foreign influences or even the personal whims of manufacturers and buyers. The Ministry therefore issued guidelines, and officially approved *tevoda* shrines can now be made only in the traditional Khmer style, meaning a square chamber with a spire, either one or three pillars at each corner, and guardian *nagas* and *garudas* on the roof. The shrine sits on a tray or platform on top of the pillar with further guardian *nagas, garudas* and lions, and around the edge of the platform there is a decorative wall made of two *nagas*, their upraised heads framing the entrance.

The shrine is called *rean tevoda*. *Rean* means a shelf, and although elaborate shrines like Leng Sophoan's are very popular, a simple shelf will do just as well. Whether dolls-mansion or simple shelf, the *rean tevoda* should be placed in a corner at the front of the house, inside the house yard and facing the house door, but not directly in front of it. This is partly so that the *tevoda* can take in the entire house, and partly because the *chumneang pteah* has her shrine inside the house facing outwards, and the two should not confront each other.

## The *Chumneang Pteah*

The *chumneang pteah* is one of the very few Cambodian spirits that is wholly benevolent. Her name means 'guardian lady of the house', and she protects the house and its inhabitants from all enemies, both supernatural and human.

The spirit is entirely Khmer, but its origins are disguised by the appearance of its shrine – a wooden box with one open side like a tiny puppet theatre, with Chinese characters across the front gable and a Chinese-looking porcelain statuette inside. Unlike the *tevoda* shrine, which is outside the house and raised on a pillar, the *chumneang pteah* is inside and on the floor. In a village house it would sit against the main house-pillar, but in modern apartments it's against a wall.

The *chumneang pteah* requires constant attention. Incense should be burnt every day, and offerings of flowers, fruit and cups of tea kept refreshed every week. The fruit can be taken away and eaten the day after being offered, but the flowers should be left in place. On special holy days a more elaborate feast is prepared, involving, usually, a roast chicken and other treats. The feast is first offered to the spirit, and later eaten by the humans of the house. Chinese-style paper offerings are also popular on special occasions, especially 'ghost money', although Cambodians don't burn the ghost money.

This is the appropriate way of installing the *chumneang pteah* in a newly built house:

Chumneang pteah *shrine with offerings on a major festival.*

Before the house goes up the central pillar is dressed in clothing and jewellery belonging to the senior female of the household, together with a stick of black sugarcane. (Sugarcane, together with rice and bananas, represents prosperity and fertility.) The house is then built around the central pillar, and its completion is marked by an elaborate inauguration in which the *achar* ties cotton threads to the wrists of the senior members of the household and around the central column, ensuring that both the spirit and the human owners of the house are tied to their homes. (A very similar ceremony is held to 'open the eyes' of a new Buddha statue as a re-enactment of his Enlightenment.)

In city apartments the shrine is simply purchased and placed on the floor facing the door if possible, so that the spirit can guard the entrance. The householder can then burn incense to invite the *chumneang pteah* to take up residence, and say a silent prayer asking for its protection. The usual offerings can then be made. The ceremony is most effective if carried out on a holy day, and a Buddhist calendar with the holy days marked on it is often taped to a wall nearby.

Chinese homes and businesses have a shrine called the *kongma*, and because so many businesses are Chinese-owned it's very common in restaurants and shops. In appearance it's indistinguishable from the *chumneang pteah*, but the *chumneang pteah* is the spirit-owner of the house and the protector its inhabitants, whereas the Chinese *kongma* are family ancestors who bring prosperity to the living in return for proper filial devotion. The *kongma* are therefore closer in meaning to the urns containing the ashes of parents, which are also kept on a shelf high up on the wall. Perhaps the easiest way to distinguish them is that the Khmer *chumneang pteah* is placed on the floor against the main house-pillar or by a wall near the front door, while the *kongma* is fixed to the wall above head height.

## The *Mrieng Kongveal*

*Mrieng* means children and *kongveal* means cowherd. In Cambodian villages the task of guarding the family's cows falls to young boys. The *mrieng kongveal* are their spirit equivalents, little spirit cowherds, although their charge extends to all useful domestic and wild animals from cows to elephants. (Animals destined for the table, such as chickens and pigs, enjoy no protection.) In the village their job is to ensure that these animals are properly treated, and if they see a farmer beating or starving a buffalo or ox they'll punish him with illness.

The *mrieng kongveal* are charming, but a Khmer ritual text called the *Hau Pralung* warns of 'the little *mrieng kongveal* with gleaming frizzy hair' who live in the forest and are 'terribly mean'. Until quite recently they were strictly rural, but within the last decade they've made a highly successful move to the city, where they seem to have lost all trace of meanness.

Their shrine looks like a bamboo dollshouse on a tray. It comes equipped with four short bamboo tubes, called glasses, which are meant to hold water for the spirits although they often seem to be used for incense sticks instead. The shrine always has miniature suits of red clothes for the spirits to wear, since the *mrieng kongveal* are naked until domesticated.

Like the *rean tevoda*, the *mrieng kongveal* is an outdoor shrine. It should hang from a bush or tree, or at the very least from a nail in the wall, but on no account should it have direct contact with the ground.

While the *chumneang pteah* and the *tevoda* will hear prayers for general good fortune, the *mrieng kongveal* are far more specific. If the householder tells them exactly what is desired – success in business or exams, a promotion at work, a new car or the latest phone – they will provide it. They ask for nothing in return, but being children they like offerings of sweets.

Mrieng kongveal *shrine*.

## The Second Shrine Merchant's Tale

Im Kim Ly has been selling shrines at Psar Chas (Old Market) for fifteen years. She once had a gold shop, but a bout of serious illness caused her to lose her business and most of her money. When she recovered she thought of shrines, as it's a field that needs little start-up capital.

She sells mostly *mrieng kongveal* shrines. She also sells *chumneang pteah* shrines, but the demand is comparatively slight and they make up no more than a tenth of her stock. Over the last ten years *mrieng kongveal* have become a must-have for Phnom Penh householders, but they are very much a Khmer shrine – the Chinese know about them but aren't much interested. Im Kim Ly puts the boom down to the many new apartments and flats being built in the city – *mrieng kongveal* shrines are cheap and easy to install – as well as to tales of how the spirits have brought prosperity and good luck to those who provide them with a home.

Prices have also boomed, likewise architectural exuberance. The largest look like city townhouses, three storeys tall and festooned with balconies and external staircases. The simplest sell for about five dollars, but the most expensive she ever sold – a private order – cost the buyer a thousand dollars.

The *mrieng kongveal* appear in dreams as naked little boys asking if they can come and play. If told to go away they'll probably continue pestering until they get permission to stay. Incense should be burnt and offerings of sweets and small toys left on the tray to welcome the child-spirits into their new home. It is possible that the spirits might fail to come, or even leave the shrine. This will be signalled by a run of bad luck or illness, and in this case an expert on the spirit world must be consulted to find the cause and make a remedy.

Im Kim Ly half believes in the *mrieng*, because customers have told her they've seen them, but she also half doesn't, because she's a Buddha-follower and believes that everything in life is the result of good and bad actions. Believing half in the magical world and half in the Buddha world creates problems for Kim Ly. Her son and his girlfriend share the same animal (meaning they were both born in the same animal zodiac year), and this is bad. She believes she should forbid the marriage for their own good, "but I can't even kill a fish, so how could I separate my son from his girlfriend?"

A monk once told her that the name of the *mrieng kongveal* was originally *abrok abronh*, a very common phrase in the countryside but one not used in the city. The monk also told her that these are the spirits of human children who have died.

# 9 Earthly Powers

*The* boramey *spirits are the Cambodian equivalent of patron saints,
providing protection to worshippers and a means of contacting the
spirit world. Their human vehicles are the* kru boramey. *These are
the shamans of the Cambodian spirit world.*

## Kru Boramey

The *boramey* are powerful spirits who act as intermediaries between the human and
supernatural worlds. They do this through the *kru boramey,* their human representatives,
who lend them a physical body. An anthropologist named Didier Bertrand spent three
years interviewing both the *boramey* and the *kru,* and what follows is based heavily on
his work.

Almost all *kru boramey* are female. The career of a *kru boramey* usually begins with a
period of inexplicable ill health, and frequently a prolonged period of unconsciousness.
This marks the period when the spirit chooses her, but often she fails to understand
what is happening until an experienced *kru* identifies the cause.

Having learned the cause of her ill health and unconsciousness, she must next find out
the identity of the *boramey.* The *boramey* will make this known through its behaviour.
For example, if the *rup* (body) trembles continually while possessed, she might be
hosting Hong Mea, the Golden Stork, who trembled with cold when stripped of her
golden feathers; if she makes swimming motions, it might be Tep Macha, the divine fish.
Other *boramey* will make themselves known by their preferences in food and clothing,

or by their speech, or the ritual objects they prefer. Often the *boramey*'s preferences will be quite contrary to the normal lifestyle of the *kru* – an abstemious and decorous human might be chosen as the *rup* of a *boramey* who likes to drink rice wine, for example. In any event, becoming a fully-fledged *kru boramey* involves a long apprenticeship.

The *boramey* demand the highest standards of behaviour from both *kru* and client. Grateful clients press donations on their *kru*, but the *kru* usually passes these to the local monastery in recognition that the teaching of the Buddha is the supreme truth. A venal *kru* who becomes wealthy from donations cannot expect to retain a large following.

There are said to be 10,000 *boramey* in Cambodia, although I doubt there's been a census. Most are Khmer but many are Chinese, Siamese, Lao or Javanese, and there is even said to be a Frenchman who has become a *boramey*, although Didier Bertrand never met this spirit. Here are just a few: Om Vathey, who was formerly the Hindu goddess Parvati; Champoh Krud, formerly one of the divine eagles who guard Mount Meru; Neang Chek and Neang Chom, twin *boramey* highly revered in Siem Reap; Preah Koh, the sacred cow and his brother Preah Keo; Neang Neak the *naga* princess, wife of the founder of the Khmer race; Khleang Moeung, the saviour of his country, who may or may not have been a real historical person; and the indisputably real Krapun Chouk, the beloved infant daughter of King Sihanouk who died suddenly at the age of four and has a *chedey* for her ashes in the grounds of the Silver Pagoda next to the royal palace.

Although it seems that anyone and anything can be a *boramey*, there are certain limits. Many *kru* will deny that heavenly beings such as Indra, king of the gods, and Maya, the mother of the Buddha, could ever be *boramey*, being too exalted to return to this world; but these beings have *kru* who reply that the highest *boramey* are the best, although they do not enter their human *rup* but merely visit and give advice – perhaps a reference to a state of meditation which brings visions of supernatural beings.

Village *neak ta* are too lowly to be *boramey*. However, as one medium explained to Didier Bertrand, village *neak ta* who wish to aid humans can study to improve their knowledge of religion and take an exam in order to become *boramey*.

The last 30 years have seen a great increase in *boramey* and *kru boramey*. Many *kru* put this down to the fact that so many good and virtuous people died without proper funeral rites in the Pol Pot period and after. These spirits are now seeking out humans to help spread their teachings.

Sometimes an inexperienced medium will be possessed by an evil spirit instead of a *boramey*. Experienced *kru* explain that this can happen if the novice has done the

*Neang Chek and Neang Chom, guardians of Siem Reap.*

meditation wrongly or violated the state of virtue required of a *kru*. But even evil spirits can be educated and transformed into low-ranking good spirits. This is rather similar to the way village *neak ta* can rise to the status of *boramey*, or even more so to the way the malevolent *bray* can become the tame guardian of a boat or Buddha statue, so that the distinction between good and evil beings does not appear to be a permanent one.

The remainder of this chapter describes the lives and powers of a handful of the most famous *boramey*.

## Sdech Kamlong, the Leper King

In the late 19th century French archaeologists at Angkor discovered a statue of a squatting, bare-chested man, his right hand apparently once holding a rod or similar object, on a terrace next to the Bayon temple. Presumably it had been there for centuries, as the terrace was used in ancient times for royal cremations and perhaps for judgements. The statue, according to its inscription, was Yama, the god of death and judgement, but the local villagers were worshipping it as Sdech Kamlong, the Leper King, who, as legend has it, was Preah Thong, the Indian prince who married the *naga* princess and was first to rule over the Khmer people.

Preah Thong was warned by his wife's father not to build a four-faced tower in his city, but he ignored the warning. Using the magical power of the four faces he captured the *naga* and imprisoned him inside the tower, but the serpent escaped and sought to kill Preah Thong. Each dealt the other many grievous wounds, but Preah Thong eventually dealt the fatal blow although he was stained by the *naga's* venom. The dying *naga* warned him not to remove the poison, but Preah Thong washed his body, and so was stricken with leprosy.

Seeking to cover up the sign of his crime from his queen, the *naga's* daughter, Preah Thong killed a monk, thinking he could be reincarnated in the monk's healthy body. This was a crime even worse than killing his father-in-law, and his outraged courtiers banished him to the forest, while his city became the haunt of monkeys and tigers. Eventually, after many trials, he was cured by the power of the sacred waters of the Siem Reap River and restored to his city and his throne.

The legend of the Leper King and the abandoned city is an allegory of the fall of Angkor and a hope for national salvation. However, the story is certainly older than the fall of Angkor, for the medieval Chinese traveller, Zhou Daguan mentions that a king of Angkor once fell victim to leprosy.

The statue is now in the central courtyard of the National Museum in Phnom Penh, where worshippers ask for health and prosperity as well as protection from danger. It's especially popular with students from the University of Fine Arts next to the museum, and special ceremonies with offerings of flowers and fruits accompanied by *pinpeat* music are held at New Year and Pchum Ben.

A second Leper King statue, almost identical to the first, was discovered at Angkor more recently. This is now under a bodhi tree at a traffic roundabout near the royal residence in Siem Reap. Despite being male, it's regarded as female and worshipped as Yeay Tep, 'Lady Goddess'. The Khmer Rouge broke Yeay Tep into pieces and threw her into a pond; she was dredged out in 1985 but her head was never found, and so in 1988 she was given a new one made of cement.

Yeay Tep likes 'crucified chicken', a raw, de-boned chicken splayed on a cross, and is fond of rice wine. People ask her for prosperity in business and in their personal affairs, military leaders consult her at moments of national crisis, and bargirls make her face up with powder and lipstick, so that they too can be beautiful. Her festival, held before New Year, is a major event in the city, attended by local and national leaders, and by the royal family.

## Me Sar, the White Mother

All *neak ta*, from the humblest village grandfather inhabiting a termite mound to the great Sdech Kamlong, have annual festivals called Loeng Neak Ta ('Raising the *Neak Ta'*), where they are asked to provide their followers with health, prosperity and peace in the coming year. One of the biggest is for Me Sar, the White Mother, that takes place each year at Ba Phnom in Prey Veng province.

Ba Phnom is a hill that may have been the sacred mountain of Funan, the first Khmer kingdom. An inscription dated 629 AD describes the mountain as sacred to Shiva, and Me Sar is probably the modern incarnation of Durga, Shiva's consort, a goddess to whom human sacrifice was once offered. The last such sacrifice seems to have taken place in 1877 on the orders of King Norodom, an event described decades later to scholars from the Buddhist Institute by an old man who had witnessed it as a boy.

Norodom had recently put down a rebellion by one of his brothers; two of the captured rebels were brought to Ba Phnom after the battle. Locked in neck-stocks and followed by a large crowd, they were led around the various shrines on the mountain, taking part in rituals at each, until they arrived at the shrine of Me Sar on the north-eastern slope of the hill. They were beheaded in an open field next to the shrine. The crowd fired weapons and let off firecrackers, triggering answering fusillades from around the mountain.

The Loeng Neak Ta at Ba Phnom is growing more popular each year. Visitors from

Phnom Penh and other towns regularly go out to enjoy fair-ground rides and games, and to pray to Me Sar. Human sacrifices seem to have ended, but in 2006 a man named Van Dee told the *Phnom Penh Post* that as a boy he had witnessed the sacrifice of a buffalo. The buffalo had not been sacrificed directly, however; a man cut a nick in its neck and drank its blood, after which it was killed and the meat used for a feast for the villages.

## Yeay Mao, the Black Lady

Yeay Mao ('Black Lady') is the patron of Sihanoukville and the coast, and one of the most famous *neak ta* in Cambodia. There are statues of her at Kep, Kampot and Sihanoukville, and a gigantic one at Bokor, but her main shrine is at Pich Nil where the highway from Phnom Penh crosses the hills that divide the inland plain from the coast.

There are several versions of the earthly life of Yeay Mao. In one she's a brave virgin warrior who was victorious against invading Thai armies; in another she had a husband who drowned at sea, for which reason she hates men and takes the lives of sailors and fishermen; and in a third story she's the abandoned wife of a faithless prince, for which she hates men (again) and vows to collect two million penises in revenge.

The guidebooks describe Pich Nil as a long row of shrines on the northern side of the highway, each stuffed with wooden phalluses. The books are out of date. Devotees still offer the phalluses, but the shrine attendants collect them as soon as the devotees depart. They keep them in a cardboard box behind the main shrine, and whenever the box is full they burn them. The chief attendant explained to me, rather apologetically, that this was because they made the place untidy, but from other sources I understand that Yeay Mao has given instructions that she no longer wishes to receive this type of offering.

A few phalluses, the most interesting ones, can't be burnt. These are almost man-sized, beautifully carved from stone, with a small Shiva figure in low relief on the tip and a *yoni* at the base. (The *yoni* is the female sex organ, the female equivalent of the *linga* or penis.) Devotees pour water over the top of the *linga* and collect it as it pours out the lip of the *yoni*, having become powerfully sacralized by contact with the Shiva-linga. Their prayers are for children, and also for the restoration of male virility.

Besides phalluses, Yeay Mao's appropriate offering is bananas. From Kep to Koh Kong fishermen and their wives leave bananas on the beach, and fishermen all along the Cambodian coast hang hands of bananas on their boats. The bananas are a symbolic

*Yeay Mao, guardian of the coast, at Kep.*

substitute for the phallus, as devotees will freely explain.

Yeay Mao's other function is to offer protection for those in peril on the roads, which is everyone. Trucks and cars stop at Pich Nil to be doused with holy water from the sacred well of the goddess, which is now located on the opposite side of the road from the row of shrines, although it was once on the same side (the shrines, not the well, have moved). Her reputation as a patron of road-users seems to have begun in the 1980s, when the road over the forested hills between Sihanoukville and Phnom Penh was infested with Khmer Rouge guerillas.

## Khleang Moeung, the Faithful General

Khleang Moeung in his earthly life was a high military official under King Ang Chan, whose capital was at Lovek. At this time the Khmer were fighting against Siam. Ang Chan fought bravely, but the Siamese were too many. They burnt Lovek to the ground, executed Ang Chan and all his sons, and led the people off into slavery.

Among those captives was a queen of Ang Chan who was pregnant with the king's son, the last hope for the royal line of Jayavarman. She hid the identity of the child's father and he grew up in the palace of the king of Siam. He proved to be intelligent and industrious, in time becoming the head of the king's elephant army.

This youth's name was Chey Aschar. Determined to regain his father's throne and his country's freedom, he told the king of Siam of a white elephant that had been seen deep in the forests of Cambodia. This elephant, he said, could only be captured if he took with him all the king's elephant army and the king's sacred sword. The king agreed, but no sooner was Chey Aschar safely in Cambodia than he announced his true identity and called on loyal Khmer to rally round him.

But alas, only a handful answered, and among them only Khleang Moeung had any experience of fighting, he alone having escaped the sack of Lovek. Chey Aschar was in despair – how could he fight the Siamese, even with his army of elephants and the brave Khleang Moeung, if he had no soldiers?

Khleang Moeung proposed a solution, although one that would mean the sacrifice of his life. He ordered a pit to be dug and lined with sharp stakes. In seven days, he told the handful of loyal Khmer warriors, they would hear a great sound of thunder, which would mean that he had raised the ghosts of Cambodia's dead to come to their aid. Telling them to fight bravely, he and his wife and sons jumped to their deaths on the spikes.

Seven days later the army of Chey Aschar was at Battambang, facing the vastly larger Thai army, when the sound of mighty thunder was heard. The ghost army of Khleang

Moeung attacked the enemy, inflicting on them painful stomach cramps, nausea, diarrhoea and dizziness. With the Siamese unable to fight, the Khmer fell upon them and massacred them in great numbers.

That was the end of the Siamese threat to Cambodia, at least for the time being. Chey Aschar was enthroned at Lovek, and in gratitude to his loyal servant he decreed that a ceremony should be held each year in the sixth month of the Khmer calendar for *neak ta* Khleang Moeung.

Khleang Moeung's annual festival is held at Pursat, halfway between Phnom Penh and Battambang. It is attended by people from all over Cambodia, including monks, local and national political leaders, and even royalty, for Khleang Moeung is to Cambodia as Saint George is to England.

## The *Boramey's* Tale

*Tum Teav* is a Cambodian literary classic, and has been a part of the national school curriculum since the 1950s despite the fact that the story is an assault on traditional Khmer values – Tum leaves the monkhood to pursue his love for Teav, the pair sleep together without being married, Teav deceives her mother. It has been called the Cambodian *Romeo and Juliet*.

In Tbong Khmom, Tum, a handsome young monk with a fine singing voice, has fallen in love with the beautiful Teav, and she with him. Tum leaves the monkhood to be with her, ignoring the warning of his abbot that this is the way of *dukkha*. The two spend the night together, hiding their affair from Teav's widowed mother, Daun Phann. But when Tum's fame as a singer reaches the ears of the king, he is called away to serve at the court, and must bid farewell to Teav.

Daun Phann, still unaware of her daughter's love for Tum, arranges for her to marry the son of Orh-Chuon, the provincial governor. Teav protests, hiding her love for Tum, but Daun Phann tells her that "the cake should never be bigger than the basket," meaning a daughter should not defy her mother, and Teav dutifully submits.

The wedding plans are interrupted when a royal messenger arrives: King Rama has heard of Teav's beauty and wishes her to come to the palace, where he will make her his chief concubine.

When Teav arrives at the palace Tum daringly sings to the king of their love for each other. Rama turns to his new chief concubine to ask if this is true, and Teav confesses her love for Tum. King Rama, deeply touched, agrees to their marriage.

Daun Phann, who has been looking forward to becoming the mother of the chief royal concubine, does not welcome this development. She lures Teav back to the village with the intention of marrying her to the governor's son. Preparations are already under way when Tum arrives with a royal edict forbidding the wedding, but he is murdered by Orh-Chuon. Teav kills herself on his body.

When King Rama hears the news he orders the execution of Daun Phann, Orh-Chuon and Orh-Chuon's son, and all the villagers are made hereditary royal slaves.

One Cambodian chronicle places these events in the year 1654. In 1654 the king was Ramathipadi I, but his history reads more like Macbeth than Romeo and Juliet. He murdered his way to the throne, oppressed his people, converted to Islam and died in Vietnamese captivity.

There are closer parallels with an earlier king called Paramaraja, who came to the throne in 1568 and fought many battles with Cambodia's enemies between then and his death in 1579. The royal chronicles mention a disobedient provincial governor of this time named Orh-Chuon.

In 1883 a French archaeologist and scholar of folklore named Etienne Aymonier visited Tbong Khmom. The villagers told him the story was true, that they resented being known as the descendants of slaves, and that for this reason it was strictly forbidden to tell the story of Tum and Teav in their province. Aymonier was able to visit the sites of the story, including the spot where the lovers died, but had to do so discreetly and under guard.

*Daun Phann* is now a *boramey*. My friend Socheat told me about her because his mother-in-law has tried many *boramey* and swears by the power of Daun Phann and her *kru*. The *kru* is named Som. When Som was 13 she fell unconscious and remained in a coma for a week. Her parents thought she was dead, but during this time she was with Daun Phann, who told her she had a mission to perform on Earth and wanted her to be her human body. Som refused. Daun Phann loves to chew betel, but Som said that betel-chewing looked disgusting, and was only for old ladies.

Daun Phann told Som that she should agree because she, Som, was her daughter and the cake is never larger than the basket. Som asked Daun Phann how she could be her daughter, as she had a mother still living. Daun Phann said she meant that Som was the reincarnation of Teuv. (Much later in life, when Som married, Daun Phann told her that her husband was the reincarnation of Tum, but that was far in the future.)

Som didn't believe this, so Daun Phann said she would prove it. She took Som, still in her unconscious state, to a place where they both had their blood tested, and sure enough it turned out that they were related, and so Som agreed to become the *kru boramey* for Daun Phann.

When she is possessed by the *boramey* Som feels nothing and knows nothing. She isn't present. She still hates betel, but Daun Phann chews it without stop. Sometimes Som vomits after a session because of the betel Daun Phann has been chewing, but Daun Phann calls it her 'delicious snack' and is highly appreciative when clients bring it to her as a gift.

People come to Som constantly with their problems. They are poor farmers, sick people, people possessed by demons, people with mental problems, but the majority are business people. Som turns no-one away, because Daun Phann tells her she must help people. If Som tries to avoid her duties she gets sick, and sometimes she can't sleep because Daun Phann is telling her to get up because she must rescue people.

Daun Phann gives blessings and medicines to the sick, helps the undecided to make up their minds, helps those who are having difficulty having a child or who want a baby of a certain sex, and generally helps things go smoothly at home or at school or at work.

Som never does bad things. This is extremely important to Daun Phann, because of her own history with her daughter Teav, but is also in keeping with the teachings of the

*Daun Phann gives advice.*

Buddha. I asked Som if I could interview Daun Phann. Som said she couldn't speak for the *boramey*, but she'd call her and I could ask her myself.

Som put on a traditional blouse and scarf and tied her hair up in the old style in a chignon with a clip, while her husband, who had so far been sitting quietly preparing betel wads, put on a music tape. Som then sat in prayer-posture, legs bent and to one side, facing her shrine with her back to Socheat and me.

There was no visible change while Som was praying, but when she turned round to face us, sitting now in the cross-legged position of authority figures, everything was different. Som had been a typical middle-aged Cambodian housewife, rather deferential, sweet-faced, speaking in the high-pitched tone adopted by Cambodian women as a part of their femininity; as Daun Phann her eyes were piercing, her gaze level and inquisitive, her body language commanding. She looked good-tempered but slightly distrustful, and not someone to suffer fools. She addressed everyone as her grandchildren, except for her husband, whom she called her son.

Daun Phann looked first at Socheat and greeted him, then glared at me.

"Who's this?

"A foreigner," said Socheat. "He's very interested in Khmer culture and would like to interview you."

"What for? I've been interviewed before, you know. Newspapers, magazines, television, all of them. What's he want? Does he speak Khmer?"

"He's going to write a book to explain Khmer culture to other foreigners. He doesn't speak Khmer, but I'll translate for him."

"Just as well. I don't speak English. Why doesn't he learn Khmer?"

"He will, but it's not easy to learn Khmer."

Daun Phann looked me in the eye for the first time. "Good morning," she said in English. Then to Socheat in Khmer: "Well, let's get on with it. What do you want to know?"

Through Socheat I asked the spirit why she had returned to the world of humans.

"I wanted to rescue people from *panyaha* (bad circumstances), and to prove to them that I was not a bad woman as described in *Tum Teuv*, which does not represent the truth. That shows me as a bad person, but in fact I only wanted the best for my daughter, I never wanted her to commit suicide."

Our driver said he would like to ask Daun Phann for a blessing. Daun Phann asked where he was from, and he said he was from Phnom Penh.

"Aha, you mean you're from Daun Penh!" Daun Phann never refers to towns and places by their human names but only by their guardian *neak ta*.

Next Socheat asked for advice, as he was trying to decide whether to accept a new job offer. Daun Phann told him he was being looked after by two *boramey*, Daun Mao (Yeay Mao) of Sihanoukville, and Daun Yat of Pailin. These two are her colleagues in the spirit-world, and the three of them meet every month to discuss which humans they can rescue and help, because between them they know everything that people everywhere are doing. Whenever Socheat was in need he should burn incense and call the three *boramey* and explain his problem to them. "Then you will know, before the next day."

Socheat's mother-in-law told me later that she believes Daun Phann is one of the best *boramey* ever. Countless times she's seen people get what they wished for after consulting her. Usually the wishes relate to wanting a girl baby to balance a boy, or vice versa, but sometimes her predictions are more spectacular. The most memorable was a young man from Kompong Cham town who asked what the future held for him, and she said, "When you're 29 you'll be a millionaire." The boy cried out that he was only a poor man's son, but by the time he was 29 he was the owner of the biggest soft-drink and beer distribution business in Kompong Cham province and a dollar millionaire.

Daun Phann doesn't say everyone can be a millionaire. Socheat is thinking of setting up his own business, and he asked Daun Phann about this. She didn't say he'd be successful or unsuccessful, or even whether it was a good idea, simply that the best time for him to do this would be when he was 39 to 45 years old.

When it was my turn she warned me that I was too generous. This was true, as I was paying for my driver and Socheat. Then she gave me some charms and amulets, for which I offered my donation.

# 10 The Mirror of Yama

*Like all people, Cambodians have to deal with life's great transitions,*
*with birth, marriage, old age and death. Because they are Buddhists,*
*they also have to deal with reincarnation. For this reason the wheel*
*of becoming begins with death.*

## The Wheel of Becoming

Yama, god of death and judgement, attended the Buddha at his Enlightenment. He was there because the Enlightenment meant an end to *samsara*, the cycle of death and rebirth over which Yama presides.

Yama is present when every man dies, holding up a mirror to the dying soul. In the mirror the soul sees the Six Realms – the three worlds of men, gods and *asuras*, from which rebirth into a higher realm is possible, and those of animals, demons and hell-beings. Death therefore comes before birth, because death is not the end. The soul is about to undertake a journey to the realms of Yama.

The first question is, what exactly is soul?

The sage Vacchagotta asked the Buddha whether the immortal soul exists. The Buddha remained silent, and Vacchagotta asked whether the soul does not exist. The Buddha still remained silent, and Vacchagotta got up and went away.

Ananda, the Buddha's favourite disciple, asked the Buddha why he had not answered Vacchagotta.

"If I had answered: There is a soul; would that be in accordance with my knowledge that all *dhammas* are without self?"

"Surely not, Sir."

"And if I had answered: There is no soul; that would have created greater confusion in the already confused Vacchagotta, for he would have thought: formerly I had a self, but now I do not."

The Buddha always refused to answer this question. What Buddhism teaches is that the cause of rebirth is *vinnana*, meaning consciousness, or more precisely still, consciousness of self. So long as this exists, rebirth continues, but consciousness of self is a false consciousness, and a self built upon it is a false self.

*Vinnana* is a rarefied notion. Ordinary Cambodians talk about *pralung*.

*Pralung* is that which animates. It is not uniquely human. Animals have it, as do plants and even certain objects. *Pralung* is multiple – every individual has 19 according to the classic texts. The *pralung* can leave the body and return, and dreams are the records of its wanderings; in similar fashion a person who has lost consciousness is said to have lost his *pralung*, and a folktale tells how some little girls lost in the forest are scared 'as if they had lost their *pralung*'.

The *pralung* seem to be rather simple and gullible. Evil spirits seduce them into the forest with lying promises of a life of luxury and ease, although in fact the wilderness is a place of great danger. If the *pralung* listen to the voices and wander off, their human owner becomes psychically weakened, prone to bad luck and illness.

There is therefore a ritual for calling the *pralung* back to the body. It involves the incantation of a poem called *Hau Pralung* ('Calling the Souls'), one of the oldest works in Khmer literature and the most widely-performed non-Buddhist work in the Khmer language. The poem itself is the most important ingredient in the ritual, but it also involves various symbolic props which appear over and over in Khmer religious ceremonies: balls of sweet sticky rice, cones made of rolled banana leaves, sticks of black sugarcane and candles tied to leaf-shaped candle-holders, called *popil*. Some of these, like the rice and sugarcane, are symbols of domestic life, but the *popil*, which is a modern version of the ancient Shiva-linga, is plainly phallic.

A full *Hau Pralung* is extremely dramatic. It begins by invoking the protection of the Buddha, all the Meru-gods and the *tevoda* in streams and hills, then warns the *pralung* of the ghosts and evil spirits in the forest. It appeals to them to come home to 'silk mattresses and wool carpets, cushions and pillows', and ends by welcoming them back to the family. 'The 19 *pralung* have arrived and are entering their home. After three days of calling I am tying strings around your wrists to unite you with your relatives, old and young, grandmothers and grandfathers. May you recover as of today'.

## Death

A man who knows his time has come asks the monks and a wise *achar* to join his family at his bedside. The monks, whose very presence brings merit, recite the Five Precepts while the *achar* prays, reminding the dying man that his only companions on the coming journey will be the good works of the Buddha and the merit gained from his own past acts. Candles and incense are placed in his hands, and at the moment of his passing a candle is lit and he is given guidance on the path to reincarnation.

The dying man's breath ceases and his heartbeat stops, but death is not yet complete. His spirit needs to be detached from his physical remains. The corpse is washed and covered with a white cloth then placed in a coffin, and the spirit is invited to enter this new 'house' – the coffin must never be referred to as a coffin lest the spirit become alarmed. At the same time a marquee is erected in the street outside the house and a funeral feast is held, accompanied by traditional funeral music. Normally this feast lasts three days, although it can be shorter or longer depending on the means of the family.

As soon as the funeral feast ends the coffin and its body are taken to the monastery and placed on a funeral pyre for cremation. The head monk delivers an oration, the funeral pyre is lit and when the flames die down the *achar* asks, "Finished or not finished?"

Everyone replies, "Finished!"

The monks sprinkle holy water and the ashes are 'turned' (raked over). At this point the *pralung* is still present, since it cannot be consumed by fire. Small banana-leaf containers filled with rice are placed on the damp ash so the spirit can have a 'body', the ashes are mixed with sand and formed into a life-sized figure, and the figure covered first with a banana leaf, then a spirit flag inscribed with the name of the departed, so that he can identify himself to the judges of the dead. The funeral *achar* then strikes the banana leaf and flag with a spade, sending them as far off as he can, so that the spirit can begin its journey.

When all this is done the family collects the ashes and takes them back to the house, where they are kept in an urn on a shelf. On the seventh day after the death, the monks and *achar* return to the house and inform the spirit of the death of the body. The spirit hears the grieving family and tries to join them, but the *chumneang pteah* will turn it away. The ghost realises that it is now homeless. If everything has been done properly it will not be malicious and will not haunt or frighten anyone. Recognizing that it now has no earthly home it will make its way to hell, accepting that it must endure punishment and suffering in order to be reborn.

*A celestial spirit in prayer on the end of a coffin, Wat Lanka, Phnom Penh.*

Somewhat paradoxically, while the *achar* is telling the spirit to depart, the family in their private prayers will invite it to stay and offer them protection and guidance as part of the *meba*, the ancestors; Buddhism and animism co-existing harmoniously while ignoring a major contradiction.

On the 100th day a marquee is set up in the street for a second funeral feast. Those who were mourners at the seven-day feast are now celebrants, because the soul has passed from this world. Food is offered to the monks, who taste a little of each and transmit the merit of the gift to the dead as an aid in the quest for a good reincarnation.

At some point after the 100-day ceremony the ashes are transferred to the local monastery, both because here the powerful presences of the monastery *neak ta* and the tamed *bray* will guard it against evil spirits, and because the proximity of the monks brings merit for the dead.

## Rebirth

An unborn baby is an old soul. A woman might dream that a man asks her if he can come to stay, or she might be visited by her dead grandmother asking to be reborn. She should generally say yes, unless she has witnessed a fatal accident recently, in which case the visitor is probably a ghost trying to be reborn before its time.

When she becomes pregnant the village midwife and elders advise her about diet, medicines and activities. She should avoid spicy foods, as they make the baby aggressive and bad-tempered. Goose eggs will make the baby intelligent, and rice wine, herbal medicines, coconut water and beer, will all make it healthy. She should not drink milk or bathe at night, as these make for a fat baby and a difficult delivery. As a cure for morning sickness she should step over her husband, with his permission, which transfers the sickness from her to him. (For a woman to step over a man would normally be a major breach of protocol.) The gender of a yet-unborn child can be predicted by standing another baby on the pregnant mother's stomach and watching the reaction, or by the morning sickness (bad sickness predicts a boy).

Most Cambodian babies are delivered at home by the village midwife, assisted by female relatives and friends – men and unmarried girls are not allowed to be present at a birth. For a period after the birth, varying from a few days to a full month, the new mother will lie on a bamboo bed with a fire in a clay pot constantly burning beneath her. This is because she is 'cold', and her heat must be restored. Drafts, which would be cooling, are excluded, and a heated tile or stone is placed on her stomach. During this period she also eats 'hot' foods, which were avoided during pregnancy.

A wet-nurse will feed the baby for the first three days, but after that breast-feeding is favoured as it makes the baby intelligent and strong.

Great care is taken to ensure that the baby, its mother and the midwife all have their full *pralung*. Prior to the birth a *popil* (see page 99) will be turned around the pregnant mother to call the baby's *pralung*, and after the birth the mother and midwife tie cotton threads to each other's wrists and ankles to attach their *pralung* to their bodies. The midwife will 'open the eyes' and 'cut the wild hair' of the newborn and call its *pralung* to leave the forest and enter its body, after which she will tie a cotton thread with a gold ring to one wrist and a plain thread to the other – again, this is to tie the *pralung* to the body. After this is done the proper offerings will be made to the ancestor-spirits and the child can be given its name.

If the birth takes place in a hospital, the newborn will be given a spirit-kit of scissors, knife and other objects, and incense will be burnt to the spirits. When the new parents take the infant home they can draw an X on the wall or on the baby's forehead to deter evil spirits. One or two weeks later they will take it to the wat, where the monks will say prayers and sprinkle it with holy water and tie a red thread round its wrist, all for its protection.

If the infant becomes sick the parents will take it back to the monastery for further blessings and perhaps an amulet to be worn round its neck. This will be in addition to, not in place of, taking it to a doctor or clinic. In both villages and cities the infant's fontanel will be painted with rice-flour for several months after birth to close up the skull.

When the baby is a little bigger, its mother from its former life will probably come to play with it. She will be invisible to the new parents, but when she's present the baby will laugh and smile at nothing, and when she leaves the baby will be sad and cry. The former mother is generally harmless, but sometimes she loves her baby too much and makes it sick, and the new mother will need to say a prayer and ask her to spare the baby because she loves it. If the illness continues or worsens it might mean the previous mother wants to take the baby back to the spirit world; in this case the parents can hold an adoption ceremony with a third party, tricking the former mother into thinking that the infant is not hers after all. This period of supernatural visits and dangers ends at about the twelfth month.

## Childhood

In its first year the infant is the centre of constant attention and love, and for its first three or four years it lives in a warm and receptive world of permissiveness and immediate fulfilment. There is little corporal punishment. As it grows older its world becomes harsher, especially on the birth of a younger sibling. The transition from infancy to childhood is a gradual increase in responsibility and socialization. By the time the child begins school he or she will have learned such basics as respect for elders and monks. During this time also the child's father gradually turns from a warm and loving figure to one who is remote and authoritarian, although the grandfather will continue to dote on his grandchild.

The basic lessons children learn are respect, obedience and how to fit in to society. Children's games emphasize skill and cooperation rather than winning. The child's performance of its duties within the family – household chores for the girls, looking after animals and supervised farm work for the boys – attracts no praise or reward, but failure or incompetence will attract blame and scolding. The parents' control over their children is absolute, and children do not conceive of themselves as autonomous beings.

The village tradition – one rapidly dying out but not yet dead – is that a child's head should be shaved except for a forelock. At some point between the ages of seven and eleven this topknot is ritually cut in a ceremony involving the monks, an *achar* and the family, after which the child has made the passage to responsible late childhood. For girls, this was traditionally followed by 'entering the shade', a period ranging from a few days to a few months during which she remained inside the house, avoiding all contact with men and boys, practising household duties and studying feminine etiquette. There was no ritual for the entry into the shade, but the exit was marked by a ceremony in which, among other things, a man with a branch would announce himself to be an *arak* of the forest. An *achar* would ask the *arak* not to harm the girl or to keep her *pralung* in the forest, and the *arak* would promise that the girl would be allowed to have children.

The entry into the shade is rarely practised today, but young boys still enter the village monastery in a collective ceremony at about 12 years old. For a brief moment before the ordination the *pralung* of a *naga* enters the boy, and he's referred to as a *naga* until the full ordination is complete. During his time as a serpent he wears a traditional female garment (the *hul*) decorated with scales and is beautified with make-up, gold necklaces and earrings, bracelets and rings. Possibly this is meant to represent the costume of Prince Siddhartha as he renounced the palace, but there are also clear undertones of the *naga* princess.

Boys and girls past the age of puberty rarely mix. A major exception is the Khmer New Year, when mixed groups of adolescents join to play traditional games, but in general, contact between sexes in the village setting is very limited.

# Love and Marriage

In the later 19th century an anonymous French army surgeon spent a few months in Cambodia investigating the sex lives of the inhabitants. His freedom of movement was hampered by war in the countryside, but nevertheless he managed to fit in a great deal of highly relevant observation.

The leisurely process of marriage began with the betrothal. Logic suggests it must have begun a little earlier, but we'll begin with betrothal. A female go-between would informally sound out the family of the girl on behalf of the boy's family. If the response were positive, a formal delegation from the boy's family would bring presents to the girl's parents.

If the presents were accepted – no doubt there was informal negotiation beforehand – the couple would be considered betrothed.

The boy would then move into the girl's house as a kind of domestic servant. This was necessary because the couple would not previously have met (in theory anyway), and this period was for the young man to pay court to the girl. He would sleep in the kitchen, because the girl was, of course, a virgin, and would theoretically remain so until the marriage was formalized, although it was not unknown for the bride to be pregnant on her wedding day. 'Leaving a boy with a girl is like putting an elephant in charge of the sugar-cane', says the Khmer proverb.

The Frenchman doesn't describe the wedding, but an Englishman named Christopher Pym, writing a century later, does. In the 1950s, while still in his twenties, he crossed on foot from the coast of Vietnam to Angkor in search of a road built by Jayavarman VII. He spent a year in Phnom Penh brushing up his Khmer.

Marriage, Pym says, was not between two individuals but between two families. The marathon wedding took place over three days, and its main elements were a hair-cutting ceremony (symbolic rather than literal, and an occasion for bawdy jokes and songs), a meal offered to the ancestors, and the cotton ceremony, in which the girl's wrists were bound with a white cotton thread. After the thread was tied the girl began to cry, and when Pym asked why he was told it was because she was afraid of her husband. Pym doesn't say whether the crying was formal or real.

While events took place inside the girl's house the groom waited outside in a shelter. At dawn on the last day the *achar* placed a coconut flower divided into three parts on an outside altar, the three sections being called the mother, father and child. The groom bowed to each flower section in turn and entered the house, where the bride was concealed behind a curtain.

The *achar* brought the flower sections inside and the groom bowed again to them.

At the same time a musician began a bawdy song entreating the hidden girl to allow the groom to open the curtain. The curtain was drawn aside revealing the bride, and although Pym doesn't mention it, she was dressed as Neang Neak, the *naga*-princess who met Preah Thong on the mythical beach at the beginning of time.

The girl knelt beside the boy and bowed to the three flower sections, the guests seated themselves around them and circulated *popil* and candles. The *achar* blew out the candles and wafted the smoke towards the couple. The boy and girl were now wed.

The boy took the bride's scarf and allowed himself to be led to the marriage bed like Prince Thong being led to the underwater *naga* kingdom, the guests dismantled the mother and daughter flowers and threw them over the couple like confetti. Later in the morning the newlyweds would take the father flower to the village monastery, where the head monk would scatter its grain over them.

Country weddings continue to be much as described by Pym. Modern urban weddings are shorter, with the main elements being the display of presents, the thread-tying and the hair-cutting.

❧❧❧

The anonymous French army surgeon noted the 'the almost universal chastity of the women, and the modest reserve of the Cambodian men' – in other words, old Cambodia was a conservative and even prudish society, *Tum Teav* notwithstanding.

In the late 1950s the pioneering anthropologist, May Ebihara, found the girls in the village she studied were afraid of sex and of being raped or abducted, which were apparently real dangers. Both Buddhism and the spirits disapproved of fornication, and chastity continued to be the overwhelming rule. Yet there were a few cases of a lack of chastity in the village, including a girl four months pregnant at her wedding and another who was the mistress of a high official from Phnom Penh – the second girl faced considerable disapproval, as did her parents for having allowed this to happen.

Birth control is not much practised in the villages, although STDs are well understood and condoms are used for health reasons. As a result families tend to be large. Infertility is regarded as the woman's fault, and the *kru* are consulted for causes and cure. Male impotence is also regarded as a supernatural problem rather than a medical one, although in fact there are several quite serious conditions that can cause it. Abortion is very rare, since taking life is the most serious of all sins.

The village has a thousand eyes, but the facts of modern urban life have produced a new social and moral world.

# Old Age

As a man or woman grows old he or she begins to think of the inevitable. Many will voluntarily enter a monastery as a monk or *daun chi*, but even those who don't will think of gaining merit.

The most common way of gaining merit is the 'precept day'. A group of laypeople, usually elderly, gather at the monastery on the holy days of the month under the direction of a monk to swear adherence to the Three Gems, the Four Truths and the Eightfold Path. The Three Gems are particularly significant because they serve as a confession of faith in the form of 'taking refuge – 'I take my refuge in the Buddha, I take my refuge in the Dhamma, I take my refuge in the Sangha.' Those who take refuge will observe the Eight Precepts.

There is also a more elaborate ceremony for gaining individual merit. It involves paying for a feast for the monks, together with presents of robes and fans and incense. It also involves paying for *pinpeat* music, and traditional orchestras are expensive. The ceremony is held in the home, but a tent is erected outside where lay guests are fed. It's partly a sombre occasion, because it points towards an approaching death, but also a happy one, because the merit gained will sway the balance of the next incarnation.

*A roneat, part of a traditional orchestra.*

In the village the ritual begins with forming a substitute body of the person whose life is to be prolonged. A mound of rice equal in weight to the weight of the person is poured onto a white cloth (the shroud), and a skeleton constructed on it with bones of sugarcane stalks, ribs of bananas and a coconut for a head. The rice-body is wrapped in the cloth, a miniature coffin is placed on top of the bundle and bundles of scented wood are tied to the coffin for the funeral pyre.

The beneficiary then prostrates himself or herself on top of the substitute body facing the coffin, and both are covered with a white cloth symbolizing a new placenta. The cloth is then slowly drawn away symbolizing rebirth, and the miniature coffin is cremated.

## Spirit Flags

When someone dies a very tall, narrow banner on a pole is raised outside the house. It looks much like the *tung rolok*, hung outside temples to signal a festival (see page 60), but it signals a funeral and, unlike the multi-coloured *tung rolok*, it's always white. According to *achars* and monks the name of this banner is *tung aphithoam*, which refers to the third division of the Buddhist scripture, the Abhidhamma. According to laypeople its name is *tung krapoe*, 'crocodile flag'.

The crocodile flag remains in place outside the dead person's home until the cremation. Just what it means is unclear. At one level it's simply to announce the death and mark the crucial seven-day period during which the soul remains present around the house, but the humanoid appearance suggests a symbolic meaning. The pioneering anthropologist, Eveline Poree-Maspero, concluded that the crocodile was the original earth god of the Khmer, earlier than the *naga*, which is of Indian origin, and earlier than Preah Torani, who is Buddhist. Like all earth gods the crocodile is associated with water, which represents chaos, and with the underground realm, the home of the dead.

This is the legend of the first crocodile flag.

Once upon a time there was a king who had a beautiful daughter. This daughter fell ill, and the king sent for a learned abbot, famous for his knowledge of magic, to come and cure her.

The monk had an apprentice in magic, a young monk who was not wise. In the absence of his master the young monk, using magic he was not yet able to control, transformed himself into a crocodile, then found himself unable to change back. The abbot also was unable to turn him back into a human, and so he remained a crocodile.

One day the abbot was riding the crocodile to the king's palace when they met another crocodile who challenged the monk-crocodile to combat. The monk-crocodile swallowed his master to preserve him from harm, but when the battle was over and he vomited up the abbot, he found that his beloved teacher was dead.

The grief-stricken crocodile blamed the abbot's death on the princess. Swimming silently to the palace in the monsoon floods he found her bathing with her hundred handmaidens, swallowed her and swam off. The distraught handmaidens rushed to the king, who sent his men in pursuit, but although they captured the crocodile and cut open its belly it was too late, the princess was dead.

The grieving king cremated his daughter and built a stupa on the spot for her ashes. Beside the stupa he built a monastery, burying one of the handmaidens under each of its hundred columns and hanging the crocodile's hide on a pole by the head in front of it. This was the origin of the crocodile flag.

The Pagoda of a Hundred Columns is in Kratie province, in Keng Brasath village of Sambor District some 35 kilometres (22 miles) north of the provincial capital. In times long past it was the capital of Chenla, one of the earliest Khmer kingdoms. The temple has been reconstructed several times and is not original, but the stupa of the princess is there and was the home of a powerful *boramey*. King Sihanouk used to consult her *kru* until, in 1969, she informed him that he was about to be overthrown. The *kru* disappeared soon after in mysterious circumstances.

In the early days of March 1970 people began reporting sightings of a white crocodile in the Mekong in front of the royal palace, which was an evil omen. On 18 March 1970, with Sihanouk absent from the country on an overseas visit, the President of the National Assembly read a brief announcement on the radio to the effect that Cambodia would henceforth be a republic. One of the world's oldest continuous monarchies had been overthrown. When Sihanouk's mother, Queen Kossamak, heard this she drew the royal sword, Preah Khan, from its scabbard and found that the blade was stained with blood. A few days later the white crocodile came out of the Mekong and roamed along the riverbank opposite the palace.

# The Second Nun's Tale

Plong Chanthou is 79 years old, a widow and lives in Wat Sampov Meas in Phnom Penh. She was born in Battambang province and moved to Phnom Penh when she married. In 1975 the Khmer Rouge evacuated her family to Battambang, but to a different district from the one she was originally from. During this time she lost all her four children, three girls and a boy, plus her beloved husband, who had been a civil servant for the Lon Nol government. First he was forced to work, then he was killed.

Immediately following liberation in 1979 she ran into the forest and ate wild fruits and roots to survive. After three weeks she made her way back to her village, but found that her parents' home had been appropriated by soldiers. So she walked all the way to Phnom Penh to look for the house she had owned with her husband, but that house was also now occupied by others.

She ended up living with relatives, but they treated her badly. She was suffering deep depression after the Pol Pot years and her losses and had no wish to find a job, so she helped in the house like a servant in exchange for meals. It was a bitter time. Eventually she went to live at Wat Champa monastery in Ken Svay district in Kandal Province, and later at Dombok Kpuos, before finally settling at Wat Sampov Meas in 1993.

Wat Sampov Meas is now her home. She gets up at 4 a.m. to clean, sweep and cook breakfast for herself and the monks, then she prays and serves the monks breakfast, after which she washes the dishes. Breakfast is no sooner out of the way than she prepares, cooks and serves lunch and washes dishes again, and prays once more in the evening. She follows the Eight Precepts and never eats dinner.

She has her own room in the monastery, away from the monks, cooks her own food and boils her own water. She never eats her meals in the monastery as she believes that being able to live there is more than enough, but lives on donations and gifts. Her younger brother sometimes gives her money, and some of her old friends and classmates also help regularly.

She worries about old age. "When I get really sick and unable to help the monks, I will ask my niece in Battambang if I can live with her and ask her to look after me. I know that she is kind and will take care of me before my departure (death). I never want to bother the monks or anybody at the temple." She believes that due to her good deeds her niece will arrange a good funeral for her when she dies.

Since 1979 she has had no other passion besides learning about Buddhism and doing good things to gather merit for the next life. "This life has been most unfortunate and lonely and miserable for me. My good deeds in this life should help me to avoid that fate in the next life. People tell me I should file a complaint with the Khmer Rouge War Crimes Tribunal to seek justice for losing my family, but what use is revenge? I tell them I would only do this if it could bring my children and husband back to be life again."

# 11 The Dead

*Animism provides the ritual background for birth in Cambodia and legend for marriage; Buddhism, however, is indispensible for dealing with death and the dead.*

## Hungry Ghosts

The path of reincarnation is determined by the state of the conscious mind at the moment of death. This is why the dying man surrounds himself with monks, *achars* and proper ritual. Through these he dies with a collected mind and goes to the 'peaceful place', where his stay will be short and followed by rebirth good into a good family.

Pity those who die without the chance to compose their minds, the suicides who take their own life, the victims of murder and traffic accidents, women who die in childbirth, and all others like them. They are doomed to become *kmouch*.

*Kmouch* aren't even aware that they're dead. They stay in the world of men and come to the living in dreams, bewildered and confused, asking what's happened to them and why they can't continue with their lives as before. The sun freezes them, the moon burns. They become malicious, haunting the place where they died, trying to trick pregnant women into giving them rebirth, causing accidents and disasters that will bring a similar fate on the living.

The ghost is a being with a huge distended belly, a tiny mouth and a long thin throat like a straw. It is constantly hungry. It feeds on pus, blood and filth, but can swallow almost nothing, and what does get into its mouth turns to ashes and dung. This is not punishment for past sins but because it continues to cling to the world. In a metaphysical sense the ghost is hungry for the conscious mind's stream of awareness.

## The First Ghost's Tale

*The Hungry Ghost for Sandwiches* is a modern story for young adults by Dawn Dim. It tells of 16-year-old Davan, 'a stubborn and lazy boy', not fond of study and addicted to pleasure. He takes drugs, hangs around in shopping malls with his friends, and rides his motorbike fast and without a helmet. One day just before Pchum Ben, riding dangerously as usual, he has an accident and is killed.

For six days his soul whirls around looking for food, growing hungrier and hungrier. On the seventh day he returns to his house and sees his mother crying. The Guardian of Hell (the god Yama) is waiting. "Boy!" cries the Guardian. "What are you doing here? Time you went to hell!"

Davan tells the Guardian he misses his parents, and he's hungry.

"Hungry for what?"

Because Davan is a modern boy he has modern tastes. "I want to eat sandwich! I'm dying for sandwich!"

The Guardian takes pity on Davan, who never intended to hurt anyone and was foolish rather than wicked. "Very well, I'll let you stay on Earth and you can ask living people for food. But there is one condition: you must never seek pleasure!"

Pchum Ben begins and Davan sees his parents preparing food. He follows them to the monastery and finds the *preah vihear* filled with candles and incense, and the smell of noodles, curries, cakes and soup, but there are no sandwiches, because nobody offers sandwiches at Pchum Ben.

Davan leaves the *preah vihear* and sits weeping by the boundary wall, the place where ghosts gather, remembering KFC and feeling sorry for himself. He thinks of the friends in life who have deserted him in death, and then of Lekhena, a kind girl who had always advised him to be good.

Davan goes to Lekhena's house. The dogs start howling, because dogs can see ghosts, and Davan howls with them, calling Lekhena's name.

Lekhena comes to the window. "Davan!" she cries, not realising he's a ghost. "What are you doing here? Your clothes are ragged and you look so thin and hungry!"

Kind-hearted Lekhena takes Davan to the kitchen, where the lids fly off the pots, the refrigerator opens by itself, and a plate and spoon and fork tumble out of the cupboard and land on the table. Lekhena is oddly unperturbed and starts preparing a snack. "You can eat if you're hungry. What do you want?"

"Sandwiches!" says Davan. "I want sandwiches!"

"I don't have the ingredients, but I'll prepare it for you tomorrow, just let me know what time you'll come."

Davan agrees to come back the next day. "Don't forget me," he says as he walks out the door – and Lekhena sees that he has no feet. "I'll be back!" – and Lekhena sees a skull instead of a face.

"Kmouch! Kmouch!"

Lekhena's mother comes running. "What is it? What's the matter?"

"It was Davan! He died two weeks ago! He came to me in a dream and told me he wants sandwiches!"

Lekhena's mother knows what to do. "Tomorrow morning you have to prepare food and buy sandwiches. Take the food to the monks, and in the evening put the sandwiches in front of our house on a banana leaf with three incense sticks and make an act of volition to offer it to him. That's what you must do."

Next morning Lekhena takes the food to the monastery, where she prays for Davan and a monk ties a cotton thread around her wrist, then she goes home and offers the sandwiches and incense as her mother told her.

The ghost of Davan, fed at last, is happy and freed from his whirling. After Pchum Ben he reports to the Guardian, who takes him to hell and teaches him to give up pleasure and drugs and to study and have a good character, and in due course Davan is ready for rebirth.

## The Second Ghost's Tale

Davan became a *kmouch*, a haunting ghost, because he died suddenly and violently, without time to calm his mind. Fortunately for Davan he had living people who loved him and looked after him in death, and because they fed him he was happy and handed himself in to the Guardian who took him to hell. Hell might not seem like a good place to be – its inhabitants are doomed to thousands or even millions of years of exquisite torment involving demons with red-hot tongs, thorny trees that have to be climbed every day, and much more – but at least there the ghost can begin the long process of education and improvement that leads to rebirth. A ghost in hell is called a *praet*.

Let us assume that you're Davan's mother or father. Naturally you want your son to be a *praet*, not a *kmouch*, but how can you find out his fate? You go to a *kru* who can contact the dead through her spirit.

I met a *kru* named Yeay Yom who specializes in this. She told me she needs to know how the death happened, and when and where, and most importantly the deceased person's name, because there are many millions of ghosts and even the most powerful of spirits needs to know who they're looking for.

With this information Yeay Yom enters into a trance and makes contact with the *tevoda*. I was rather surprised by this, as it was the only time I heard anyone refer to the *tevoda* outside the New Year celebrations. The *tevoda* make inquiries in the spirit world. Sometimes the soul might be in hell or even in the 'good place', but the news is not always good, and the *tevoda* might very well report that a boy like Davan is a *kmouch*. Sometimes the dead *kmouch* itself will enter Yeay Yom, distraught and confused, unable to understand what has happened, speaking through her mouth and begging for help.

Sometimes the living can feel the presence of the dead without the help of a *kru*. Pisei lost both parents when he was a child, and he grew up in an orphanage. "I think my father is reborn, because I don't feel him with me," he told me. "But I don't think my mother is reborn yet, I feel her with me all the time."

A delay in rebirth can be explained in many ways. Perhaps the soul, like Pisei's mother, wants to stay and watch over her child, or perhaps the soul's *kamm* was too much to be overcome by a good death and it has become a *praet*.

*Praets* are to be pitied, not feared. They've begun the slow accumulation of merit and can work their way to rebirth; they won't harm the living. The *kmouch* are a different case. Instead of going to rebirth or to hell, they linger on earth and become vicious. Humans who see them are afraid, their fear causes them to make offerings, but this merely develops the *kmouch*'s appetite for more offerings, and so the haunting worsens.

When Socheat's wife's sister was 19 she moved to Phnom Penh from her parents' home in Kampong Cham and rented a haunted house at Black River, which is the local name for a stinking open sewer. She was aware that the house was haunted, but the combination of the Black River at the front door and a ghost inside made it cheap, and she believed she had sufficient *reasey* (luck, a form of merit) to protect herself and those who lived with her.

There were five people in the household, the other four being her two sisters and an aunt and uncle. Perhaps the ghost decided to attack the head of the house first, or perhaps she was simply more susceptible. At any event, soon after they all moved in she was in the kitchen one day when she saw somebody coming down the hall toward her, although the front door was closed. The figure vanished, and she cried out. Everyone came running, but there was no sign of any intruder in the house. Her sisters and her uncle and her aunt told her it just her imagination, but after that she constantly felt someone watching her, especially as she was drifting off to sleep.

Then her hair started falling out.

She went to the doctor and had tests, but science could find no physical cause. She went to her mother, who told her the *kmouch* was the cause. Her mother called on the monks of Wat Botum, who are renowned for their ability in this regard, to conduct a ceremony at the house. This was not to chase the ghost away, but to ask the spirit to leave and stop causing fear to humans.

The ceremony was held, but the ghost remained. This sometimes happens, as the monks are simply asking the ghost to depart, not forcing it to do so. There is another ceremony that 'burns' the ghost, meaning destroys it, but monks cannot do this as the First Precept prohibits them from harming any beings, even ghosts. There was no option but to go to a *kru boramey*, for only the *boramey*, as a high spiritual power itself, has sufficient strength to deal with a supernatural being.

The *boramey*, speaking through the *kru*, advised Socheat's mother-in-law that it would not burn the ghost – the sin would be very great, equivalent to taking a life, and it did not wish to take this responsibility upon itself. It would remove the ghost without committing murder.

It was all over quite quickly. The *boramey* entered the *kru*, searched Socheat's wife's sister's body for the ghost, seized it and wrenched it out. The *kru* then sent her home with amulets and holy water to be sprinkled through the house while asking the *kmouch* to go to the proper world of ghosts. The girl's hair grew back, and the house remained free of haunting as long as the family lived there.

## The Festival of Hungry Ghosts

In order to be reborn the soul must accumulate merit. The hell-guardian tells Davan to give up pleasure-seeking and to study and have a good character, but how does he do that in hell? As a ghost his options are very limited, but fortunately the living can transfer merit to the dead. They can do this at any time by an act of volition – through prayer, for example – but the primary occasion is the festival of Pchum Ben, the Rice-Ball Gathering.

Once a year Yama, the king of hell and judge of the dead, opens the gates of the underworld for 15 days and allows the dead to return to the land of the living. For these 15 days, or rather nights, the living devote themselves to helping the dead. It's largely invisible to the visitor because everything important takes place at around four o'clock in the morning, but for Cambodians it's the most important religious event of the year, more so even than New Year.

This is what happened at Wat Lanka on the third night of Pchum Ben.

The main gate was flanked with vendors selling bundles of crisp hundred-riel notes, each worth about two and a half cents, plus lotus flowers and plated offerings topped with small spirit-flags. Past these, the gate itself was lined with beggars, quite a few of them small children despite the hour. The beggars seemed to be wearing their best clothes, in keeping with the dignity of the night.

The festival was taking place in the main shrine hall, which was ringed with burning candles in aluminium basins sitting on blue plastic chairs. Inside the hall the monks sat along the south wall and the worshipers along the north, separated by a long table of formal fruit-offerings topped by small spirit-flags of coloured paper.

I've always liked the altar at Wat Lanka, it's not crowded or tacky (by our standards) and the four main images are handsome. The main Buddha image was brilliantly illuminated at the west end of the hall – it shows the Buddha sitting in meditation on the Diamond Throne in the earth-touching pose; the left hand palm-up in the lap and the right bent over the knee, calling Preah Torani to witness his right to the throne. At the feet of the earth-touching Buddha was a reclining Buddha, showing him at the moment of his death and nirvana (see page 11), and on each side a tall standing Buddha with both hands raised, palms outward, in the gesture of dispelling fear.

At the east end of the shrine hall, which is always the main entrance, a traditional

*Pchum Ben – offerings to the dead, Wat Lanka, Phnom Penh.*

orchestra was ready with gongs and drums. The musicians were very young, little older than children, and they looked bored – their turn would come later.

Arriving worshippers knelt and made a prostration towards the Buddha, then sat in prayer with legs out to one side – only monks sit cross-legged. While doing this, they were making a mental act of intention directed at a particular ancestor or group of ancestors, asking that the merit about to be generated be received by them.

Meanwhile the monks, in dignified orange rows, chanted texts concerning the Three Gems, the Four Truths and the Eightfold Path. The chief monk then chanted the Pali text that establishes Pchum Ben, a quite touching poem about the loneliness and suffering of the dead and their need for the generosity of the living.

The worshippers responded with the Pali equivalent of 'amen', and a monk outside the east door began beating a huge drum. This is the traditional means of calling monks to eat, but on this night it was calling the ghosts to the feast.

As the drum was beating the *vihear* emptied and the congregation gathered outside the east door with candles, plates of offerings, spirit flags, bottles of water and bundles of hundred-riel notes. When everyone was assembled they placed the candles on the pavement and knelt in front of a row of white-shirted *achars*, joining their hands in respect as the chief *achar* explained the transfer of merit: the dead, seeing the selfless intention of the living on this night, would feel joy in the act of another's giving, and this joy would advance their moral regeneration. He then finished with another brief address on the proper way to conduct the ceremony.

The monk struck the drum again, the orchestra began playing and the head monk, still inside the shrine hall, began a chant describing the *kamma* that leads to the state of the *praets*. The central part of the ceremony now began as the congregation started circling clockwise round the ring of candles that enclosed the *vihear*. The procedure was comparatively simple: each person placed a few hundred-riel notes in each saucer, dropped a rice-ball in the basin and poured in a little water. While doing this they made a mental act of giving to a named departed person who was to benefit.

After three complete circuits the main business of the ceremony was finished and the worshippers headed for the gate. As they did so they detoured to a bamboo enclosure in the main courtyard where a stupa had been built of sand, its five peaks decorated with spirit-flags. Each one added a little sand and a few hundred-riel notes and made a prayer. At the gate they gave what notes remained to the beggars, and then went home.

Each family will repeat this at six different monasteries over six of the first fourteen nights, finishing with a seventh ceremony on the most important night, the fifteenth.

Presents and honour are also given to parents at Pchum Ben, so it's traditional to go home to villages for the last three days, which frequently means visiting the villages of two sets of parents. Phnom Penh is deserted for these three days. The generosity of the visitors from the city isn't limited to parents: they will make special efforts to be generous to all their relatives in the country, bringing gifts of food and hosting banquets, receiving in return special positions of honour in the village temple.

The cost of each night's ceremony – the hire of the orchestra, gifts and breakfast for the monks, and much more – is considerable, and sponsoring a night of Pchum Ben, whether in the city or the home village, is an opportunity for a person both to gain merit for the sponsor and to bolster his social and possibly political connections with the village.

The rice-ball is made of sticky rice and sesame mixed with coconut cream. Ghosts can only eat foul things – blood, pus, rotten fish-heads, cow dung – and so the balls have traditionally been thrown into the monastery courtyard to ensure that they are properly dirty. Today the monastic authorities are concerned about hygiene, so the abbots and achars now ask for the balls to be thrown into the baskets instead, the baskets being coated with filth in order to make the food attractive for the ghosts. This was one part of the instruction the chief achar was giving. Another important part was telling people to take the ceremony seriously and not to infringe morality – Pchum Ben has become very popular among young people in recent years, but for reasons that have little to do with piety towards the dead and much to do with darkness and deserted courtyards.

The ghosts are not thought to eat the rice-balls, any more than the dead in a Western cemetery are expected to smell the flowers. The significance of the act lies in the intention. Selfless giving generates merit for the giver, and Pchum Ben redirects the merit to the dead, for the sake of their rebirth.

Which, of course, is not to say that a lot of people might not interpret the giving of food quite literally. There's a polite but grim tussle between the monks and the laity over just how the festival should be celebrated, with the monks saying that throwing rice away is a waste of food and attracts rats and dogs, while the people are determined to help the dead, because you never know whether or not your own ancestors are working their way to rebirth.

# 12 The Four Faces

*Kingship has always been central to the Cambodian identity, and the city of the king is a ritual centre as much as a political one. This chapter traces the history of Phnom Penh, City of the Four Faces, and the concept of royalty.*

## King Jayavarman VII

Jayavarman VII was about 25 years old on the death of Suryavarman II, the builder of Angkor Wat, and in his sixties when he became king. He went on to reign for almost 40 years, expanding the Khmer empire from the South China Sea to the edge of Burma.

He was a Buddhist, though exactly what sort of Buddhist is disputed. Probably it was some form of tantric Mahayana, tantra being an esoteric Indian teaching involving union with the godhead through mysticism and magic. Certainly he was a world-ruler, and as such he probably expected that he was preparing the way for the Buddha-to-be, the Fifth Buddha. Whatever his beliefs were, he gave them form in stone in his city of Angkor Thom, just north of Angkor Wat.

Like Angkor Wat, the city was a model of the cosmos, but far larger. It forms a square with a moat and walls each three kilometres (nearly two miles) long. Each wall has a gate large enough for an elephant and rider, and over each gate is a huge tower with four smiling faces, each oriented towards one of the compass points. The motif of enigmatic smiling faces, over 200 of them, is repeated on the towers of the temple of Bayon at the centre of the city.

Nobody knows exactly what these massive, serene faces were meant to be. They might be portraits of Jayavarman himself as a divine being, and perhaps they are. The divinity Jayavarman associated with his military campaigns was the Bodhisattva Avalokiteshvara ('he who looks down in compassion'), whose statues have multiple radiating arms and tiny Buddhas filling every pore of the skin. Jayavarman sent statues of Avalokiteshvara to all the major cities of his empire, because the king was the World Ruler and his compassion lay in bringing all beings under the World Empire, where they would be able to achieve salvation.

The Bayon, like the central spire of Angkor Wat, has a well falling from a chapel at the peak to a cell deep in the interior. When archaeologists excavated this they found the original main statue of the Bayon, an image of the Buddha in meditation under the hoods of the *naga*-serpent in the last week of his meditation after Enlightenment. It had been broken into pieces and thrown down the shaft in antiquity.

In the inner gallery of the Bayon, on the north-east corner, is a series of carvings thought to have been made shortly after Jayavarman's death and showing scenes as follows:

A king and queen are in a palace, the king battling a *naga* as onlookers watch; next the king, having defeated the *naga*, sends servants to the forest in search of a healer; next women examine the king's hands; the kings reclines on a couch, apparently sick, while a wise man stands at his head; and finally a female figure, apparently a goddess, is released from a cave or temple.

This is almost, though not quite, the legend of the Leper King (see page 88).

The shrine of Preah Ang Doung Kar, the Sacred Royal Flagpole, is on the Phnom Penh riverside opposite the Royal Palace. This is probably the most popular shrine in the city, but its history is mysterious. According to a legend that appears in many variations, a pole bearing a crocodile-flag once rose up from the river at this spot on Buddhist holy days, and the people asked it to come ashore and stay with them, which it did. The more mundane explanation is that in the 19th century the royal standard was flown here to show ships coming up from Saigon (Ho Chi Minh City) where they should put in to the Customs post. The first has an authentic-sounding link to the sacred earth-crocodile but lacks any plausible connection with real history, while the second, though plausible, doesn't explain why this spot is sacred.

*Preah Ang Doung Kar.*

The name itself doesn't give many clues. *Preah* is an honorific and means Highness, Holiness – Preah Mohaksatr is the king, Preah Put is the Buddha. It applies also to a great many entities that wouldn't merit any title in English – Preah Chan is the moon, Preah Peay is the wind. *Ang* is a marker for divine beings, and *Doung* is a flagpole or a mast for hanging a lantern (so ships can see the Customs post at night?) *Kar* is a Vietnamese word for a flag (the boats were coming up from Saigon), but many Khmer refuse to accept that the revered national shrine could have any connection to Vietnam.

There are two shrine-houses at Preah Ang Doung Kar, and the one directly under the flagpole is the more important. It was probably built about 1913, at the same time as the Moonlight Pavilion on the palace wall opposite, but the image inside the shrine, the actual deity worshipped, is far older.

Or was older – the original dated from the period of Jayavarman VII but was destroyed by the Khmer Rouge, and the present statue is a copy. The shrine guardians say it's Vishnu, but the experts say it's Avalokiteshvara with thousands of tiny Buddha-images covering his upper torso, the manifestations of the meditating Bodhisattva as his body encompassed the whole universe. But it can't be one of the statues Jayavarman placed throughout the empire – those had eight arms, and this has only six.

Whatever the facts behind this statue and its connections to the history of Phnom Penh, it now protects all the lands where Khmer people live, not just modern Cambodia but the lost provinces of Kampuchea Krom (Lower Kampuchea, modern southern Vietnam) and Kampuchea Surin, the eastern Thai provinces bordering Cambodia.

On holy days and feast days it can be almost too crowded to move at Preah Ang Doung Kar, but on the afternoon when I visited there were just the usual street urchins, a few girls and women with cages full of tiny birds, and a handful of worshippers, most of them middle-class ladies. One of them joined her hands in prayer and turned her back to the shrine, her face towards the far bank where a Cambodian magnate is building a luxury resort and casino. Was she offering her prayer to the gamblers-to-be? In her hands she held two little birds, and when the prayer was done she threw the birds into the air and watched as they flew off towards Mr Sokha's hotel.

I talked to one of the bird-sellers. Sor has been selling birds at the flag shrine for the last ten years, which means she must have started as a very young child. Her customers are mostly Khmers and Khmer Chinese, but there are also Chinese and Vietnamese visitors. They're mostly young couples, or single young people, because the point of releasing the birds is to discover whether one's true love is true.

If the customers are a couple they purchase two birds, cup one each in their hands, face east (Mr Sokha's hotel is eastward), say a prayer and release them on the joint count of three. If the two birds fly off together, that means that they'll stay together.

Sometimes a single woman or man, but usually a woman, will buy a bird. Presumably a marriage is in doubt. Sor doesn't ask any questions.

An elderly lady is sitting on the balustrade along the river. Her name is Deuch. Before her retirement she ran a successful café and restaurant near Psar Thmei, which means New Market in Khmer, but is known in English as Central Market. (This is confusing, as there's another market called Central Market in Khmer, although in English it keeps its Khmer name and is known as Kandal Market.)

Deuch used to pray often at the shrine, and as a result her business was very successful. Khmer from America and Australia used to come because she was so famous. After retiring she moved to Vietnam because she was born there and wants to spend her last years there, but she still has her grandchildren in Phnom Penh and visits the shrine whenever she comes to see them. She prays for prosperity and happiness, and especially for health, because her health hasn't been good lately.

Her granddaughter Srey Leak, sitting beside her, doesn't speak unless spoken to, but when asked she says she never comes to Preah Ang Doung Kar except when her grandmother visits. Srey Leak has dropped out of high school to go into the tailoring business. Her grandmother very much approves. "You don't need too much schooling, it's better to be successful in business."

The other shrine is for the regional *neak ta*, the ones who double as *boramey*. Half a dozen teenage boys are burning incense and receiving water-blessings from the shrine guardians. They've come because they have an exam on Monday. They laugh when I ask them if the visit to the shrine will be enough to guarantee success. "No, we need to study!"

The boys leave and two girls arrive. They're from Svey Rieng near the Vietnamese border, and they work in a garment factory. One of them passed her final high school exam last year but lacks the money for university, so she's working at the factory until she can save enough. This is her second visit to the shrine, and she's praying for happiness and prosperity in life. "It's hard to say if I really believe," she says. "I just follow what others do." Her friend declines to make any comment.

A middle-aged woman has some birds that she's purchased. She prays and holds them over her head in the correct manner, but instead of facing east towards the Sokha Hotel she faces north. When she releases the birds one of them flies off, but the other drops to the ground and hops over to hide between my feet. It has no flight feathers and no tail feathers. Very soon it will be back in its cage, repeating the cycle.

As mentioned, the second shrine at Preah Ang Doung Kar is for the great regional *neak ta*, the intermediaries between the visible world and the invisible. Someone had to decide which images were to placed in the shrine but I have no idea who it was. Quite possibly it was King Norodom, who was responsible for most of the architecture at this place, including the royal palace, although it could also have been his successor King Sisowath, whose name is now attached to the boulevard that runs along the river and who was king when the shrine was built. Whichever king it was, there was a precedent. At the Bayon, many centuries earlier, King Jayavarman placed images of the *neak ta* in the corridors of his temple, thus uniting the regions to the crown.

## King Ponhea Yat

Wat Phnom is the symbolic Meru of Phnom Penh. It sits in a circular garden inside a large traffic roundabout, with a stupa at its centre, a temple and a *neak ta* shrine in its shadow.

The royal chronicles tell how, in the year 1372 (the chronicles are misleadingly precise with dates), the wealthy widow Daun Penh left her home at the foot of a hill beside the Tonle Sap River to search for driftwood. (In another version she was married and went to search for her husband, who, like the missing husband of Yeay Mao of Sihanoukville, was on the water in his boat; the husband never makes an appearance in the story, and both Daun Penh and the chronicler seem to forget about him from this point on.)

Daun Penh saw a koki tree in the flooded river and asked the villagers to bring it to the shore. In a cavity in the trunk (or among its branches) she discovered four bronze Buddhas and a stone image of Vishnu. Under her direction the villagers increased the height of the hill and built a *preah vihear* for the four Buddhas at the top using the wood of the koki tree. The Vishnu image was placed in a shrine beside the *preah vihear*, and a monastery was established on the western side, roughly where the U.S. embassy now stands.

The tourist literature presents this as a charming and rather simple-minded folk-tale, but it has deeper aspects. The koki tree is no ordinary tree, since only monks and kings can plant it. It came floating down the Tonle Sap from Angkor, bearing sacred images from an ancient capital about to fall. Four of them were Buddhas, mimicking the four Buddhas of the current age, and the fifth was Vishnu, the god of Angkor Wat. So although Daun Penh's husband never returned from the river, a god did. In the legend the Vishnu image is called Neak Ta Preah Chao, meaning Ancestral Spirit Sacred Commander, a name that provides no clue as to its origins, but does identify it as an ancestral figure.

The oldest building in Phnom Penh today is a stone tower in the grounds of Wat Ounalom. It dates from the late 12th or early 13th century, roughly the age of Jayavarman

VII. In comparatively modern times this was where the sacred eyebrow relic of the Buddha was kept, but before Buddhism became the religion of Cambodia it must have had some other purpose. Possibly – and this is pure speculation – there was a Vishnu statue either at the tower or on the hill before Phnom Penh became Cambodia's capital.

In 1432, again according to the chronicles, King Ponhea Yat abandoned Angkor in search of a new capital and settled at Phnom Penh. The date is almost certainly not true to real history, but neither is it really important. Whenever Ponhea Yat arrived, he built his palace at the foot of Daun Penh's hill.

The hill became a blank canvas on which Ponhea Yat could re-create the symbolic world of Angkor. He demolished Daun Penh's shrine, raised its height further and crowned it with a stupa. Hills are, of course, more than geography in the Khmer universe. Princesses fall off flying cows and turn into them, gods demand human sacrifices on them. Stupas, too, are more than towers. In their various sections – square base, bell-shaped mid-section, spire – they represent Meru and the heavens, and also the Buddha, whose meditating figure provides their ideal proportions. By demolishing the shrine and replacing it with a Meru, Ponhea Yat transformed the hill into the symbolic centre of the universe, as his royal ancestors had done repeatedly at Angkor.

*The discovery of the miraculous images in the koki tree.*

What we see today in the *preah vihear* at Wat Phnom is not four Buddha statues but a single, mountain-like column with four Buddhas sitting in caves, one on each face. Each sits in meditation under a *naga*, revealed by drawn-back curtains. These are Siddhartha and his three predecessor-Buddhas, in meditation following their enlightenment. In front of them is a large bronze statue of Maitreya, the Fifth Buddha, the Buddha to come.

Ponhea Yat's son and successor placed his father's ashes in the stupa, completing the symbolic mandala: the king was identified forever with the Buddhas on the cosmic mountain at the centre of his city, at the centre of the universe.

## King Norodom

When the Spanish and Portuguese first made contact with Cambodia in the mid-1500s their immediate concern was to convert the natives. They met with abject failure. One missionary, asked by his superiors to account for his lack of success, explained that the Buddhist monks, who were worshipped like gods, were turning the people against him. The court Brahmins were also hostile and so was the king, and as the king had eyes everywhere he was unable to do anything.

The Brahmins were presumably hostile because they feared for their own role, which was to surround the semi-divine king with the network of rituals that kept the universe in motion. Part of this was the casting of horoscopes, and I wonder if they foresaw the remarkable conversion of King Ramathipadi I, otherwise King Ibrahim, to Islam around 1642 or 1643. His motives are uncertain – according to some he fell in love with a Muslim Malay princess who turned his affections by means of magic spells, while according to others he wanted to gain the backing of the numerous Malays and Chams (the Chams had long since converted to Islam) living along the river near Phnom Penh. In any event, when he died he was cremated in the Buddhist manner, not buried as a good Muslim should be.

Cambodia's politics then and later was a game of royal musical chairs, as king followed king and the kingdom slipped out of their hands. One claimant to the throne would chase another out of the country, the loser would appeal to the Vietnamese or Siamese to restore him under foreign protection, and the latest loser would appeal to the other side.

In the first decades of the 19th century it seemed that the Khmer nation was in danger of extinction. The country now fell under the control of the Vietnamese, and while the Siamese had been brutal enough, they were at least fellow Theravadin Buddhists and,

*The Fifth Buddha: main Buddha image, Wat Daun Penh, with the Four-Faced Buddha-mountain behind.*

somewhat perversely, revered Khmer culture. The Vietnamese were not and did not. They were the heirs of Chinese civilization, and they attempted to remake Cambodia in their own Chinese image. This involved, among other things, the suppression of Theravada Buddhism and its replacement with Mahayana. They also attacked Khmer kingship, placing a queen on the throne and having her coronation follow the Vietnamese model rather than the ancient rituals of Angkor. A monk named Kai pronounced himself to be the long-awaited Fifth Buddha and launched an anti-Vietnamese uprising from his base at Ba Phnom, the home of Me Sar (see page 89).

Siam could not stand by and see Vietnam absorb Cambodia. For years the armies marched across Cambodia, devestating the landscape and emptying the villages, and it's a matter for wonder that Cambodian religion and culture managed to survive.

But they did, and King Norodom came to the throne, bearing the high-sounding titles of Khmer kingship – 'Grand King with divine feet, superior to any being, descendant of the gods and of Vishnu...'

Norodom remained king for nearly 40 years, from 1866 to 1904. His first task was to construct the royal palace, modelled on the palace of the king of Siam in Bangkok. In a break from traditional Khmer cosmology, which would have had it oriented to the four cardinal points, it was oriented primarily to the river in the Siamese and Lao manner. (It does, however, have the same five gates as the city of Angkor Thom.) Among the notable buildings in the compound, in addition to the Throne Hall, are the palace gifted to the king by the French with a letter N on the façade, which can mean both Napoleon II and Norodom, and the Silver Pagoda, whose official name is the Temple of the Emerald Buddha.

But it was not the palace that made Phnom Penh the capital of a rejuvenated Cambodia, nor its position at the Four Faces, nor any other symbolic building, but the king's presence. As the years passed his actual power slowly ebbed away to nothing, but he always remained the sacred embodiment of the nation.

## King Sihanouk

His Majesty Preah Bat Samdech Preah Norodom Sihanouk, more commonly known as King Sihanouk, was born on 31 October 1922, to Prince Norodom Suramarit and Princess Sisowath Kossamak. He was one of many princes and far from the obvious one to become king, but he was destined to be, without a doubt and for all his many faults, the towering figure of his century.

His uncle, King Monivong, had given the colonial masters no trouble. When he died in 1941 the French chose Sihanouk to be king because he was an immature playboy who cared only for cars and girls and had no interest in politics.

He quickly developed one, going out into the countryside on royal tours where he mingled with the villagers and showed a gift for the common touch, becoming genuinely loved. After the war he asked politely for independence, and when the French told him that this was not what they had in mind, he took his case to the world and gradually pressured Paris into giving up the last vestiges of control. Norodom had used the French to save his country from the Thais, and Sihanouk freed it from the French.

The French left Cambodia a Constitution, which decreed that Sihanouk could reign but not rule. This was not to his taste. He renounced the throne in favour of his father, took the title of Prince, and ruled as Prime Minister. Now began the Golden Age, Sihanouk building hospitals and schools, overseeing the rebuilding of Phnom Penh according to the plans of his brilliant young chief architect Vann Molyvann, playing saxophone in his own jazz band, and entertaining diplomats and journalists with his high-pitched giggle and imperious dignity. "Altesse!" he would snap at those who forgot.

The foreigners were charmed, but Sihanouk was in fact running a royal dictatorship, and peasants who provoked Papa might find their heads on spikes in his shiny new capital. Admittedly this only happened once, but the royal secret police were active and mysterious deaths and disappearances became increasingly common as time went on.

In 1970 his generals overthrew him, not because of his antidemocratic tendencies and latent savagery but because they thought he was soft on communism. Sihanouk, enraged, threw his considerable popular support behind the Khmer Rouge, and a movement which had up till then been a band of bandits in the jungle became a force to be reckoned with. By 1973 Phnom Penh was under siege, and in 1975 it fell.

The rest was something of an anticlimax for a man who always wanted to be in charge. He became a Khmer Rouge puppet (shades of Norodom and the French), and when the Khmer Rouge were expelled he tried to be a real king with Hun Sen, but failed. Ever the realist, in 1993 he forced or persuaded his son, Prince Ranariddh, who had just won the UN-sponsored free and fair elections by a wide margin, to give up all idea of running the country alone and form a coalition with Hun Sen: Ranariddh had the votes, but Hun Sen had the guns. It was Sihanouk's recognition that the monarchy was, after all, a symbol.

I was in a restaurant in Phnom Penh with a Cambodian friend on the night when word reached us from Beijing that Norodom Sihanouk, the King-Father of Cambodia, had died. News started spreading that his face had appeared on the moon. Crowds filled the streets to witness the portent, and along with everyone else my friend and I went outside to look. Neither of us could see the king, but many others assured us they could, and we thought it diplomatic to remain silent.

Sihanouk had been receiving medical treatment in Beijing when he died of a heart attack on 15 October 2012, 16 days before what would have been his 90th birthday. His body was brought home by his son, King Sihamoni, accompanied by Prime Minister Hun Sen, and over a million people lined the road from Pochentong airport to the royal palace.

This was not the palace of Ponhea Yat at the foot of Wat Phnom, which has long since vanished, but one constructed by King Norodom on the bank of the Mekong where it meets the Tonle Sap and the Bassac. The guidebooks all say that these rivers make the four faces that give the city its formal name of Chaktomuk, but it seems more likely, as has been suggested by Professor Ashley Thompson, that the faces are those of the four-faced Buddha who appeared first on the towers of Angkor Thom, then at Wat Phnom, Lovek and wherever else Khmer kings established themselves. The most important building in the modern palace compound is the Throne Hall, topped by a spire with four faces like the towers of Bayon, and kings sit directly under it to be crowned. Apart from this singular event, unique in the reign of each king except twice-crowned Sihanouk, the throne has no human occupant.

It was not until early in the morning on 1 February 2013 that the king's embalmed body was taken from the Throne Hall to the royal cremation ground opposite the National Museum. The two are separated by a single street, but the cortege wound through the city for six kilometres (four miles) so that all Phnom Penh could say farewell.

The coffin left the palace through the Victory Gate in the east wall next to the Moonlight Pavilion, where Sihanouk used to hold nocturnal performances of classical Cambodian dance in the days when he ruled Cambodia. From there it moved down Ponhea Yat Avenue to the shrine of Preah Ang Doung Kar on the Mekong, where cannons fired a salute and Brahmin priests blew silver-mounted conch shells.

The procession included the king's widow and son, Buddhist clergy including the heads of the two branches of the Sangha, representatives of the Cham, Malay and Chinese communities, and more monks than I would care to count. Last came the chariot and the coffin, the sandalwood and the sacred fire.

Led by flags representing nation, religion and king, through streets lined with crowds, it moved north up Sisowath Quay to Wat Phnom, made a semi-circle around the base of the hill, and moved south down Norodom Boulevard to the Independence Monument, designed by national architect Vann Molyvann to mark independence from France in

1953. From there it travelled east down Sihanouk Boulevard towards the Mekong and finally north again to the royal cremation ground, the Veal Preah Man.

The coffin rested in the cremation ground until, on the evening of 4 February, at the auspicious moment chosen by the royal astrologers, King Sihamoni lit the pyre as Brahmins blew conch shells and a ceremonial salute boomed out over the Mekong. The crowds, kept at a distance, were now allowed in to the Veal Preah Men and the park, where they watched replays on giant screens until late into the night. Next day a part of the late king's ashes was scattered on the river from a barge decorated with *nagas*, and the remainder was taken in an urn to be enshrined inside the palace.

A statue of the king stands next to the Independence Monument in Hun Sen Park. "They chose me because they thought I was a little lamb," Sihanouk wrote of the French. "They were surprised to discover that I was a tiger."

# 13 Inside the Crocodile

*Given that Buddhism teaches non-violence and the spirits uphold morality, how can we explain the Khmer Rouge years, the years of the crocodile?*

## The Survivor's Tale

This story was told to me one evening at a dinner after a conference in 2003. The speaker is a senior official with a Cambodian government authority. Someone asked him what it was like for him during the Khmer Rouge period.

I worked in Kompong Thom under Lon Nol regime, on staff of the Ministry of Rural Development and Refugees. I was married in 1975 January, and after two months the Pol Pot win the war. They take people outside the town to the countryside to be rice farmers. At this time I am living with my wife and my baby daughter in a village called Mango Island in Kompong Thom province, near the village of my wife parent.

They order me to plough the field for the rice, far from the village, maybe 10 kilometres, but I cannot control the buffalo. Then they bring us back to a place two kilometres from Mango Island and tell us to plough there, and after that they make a new move, but this time not normal, bring no bags, and my skin is feeling goose bumps. I fear maybe they bring me to kill, and the Pol Pot chief is there with three guards, and one guard has a knife and an axe, because Pol Pot they not shoot, they kill by a knife and an axe.

When we come to the place there are twenty of us, they have our names. The chief of the Pol Pot, he says the Organization will provide us each a white suit today. They start to call us into the room, one at a time. I say to the guard, "Oh, I say, I am stupid, I forgot my bag, someone will find it." So he thinks that someone will find my bag and they will know what has happened, so he says to me to go quickly and get my bag. I run and when I am out of sight I jump down into a hole (an irrigation ditch, two metres deep and perhaps two kilometres long).

So I jump down into the ditch and I run. I run bent over, no one can see. I run and I run until I come to the end of the ditch, then I walk along the national road to the village of my wife parent. When I tell them what has happened, at first they not believe me, they want me to go back to Mango Island, but after they see that I am so frightened they believe me. They make me some rice and my wife brother write a letter saying that I am ordered by Organization to go to work on the ditch in another place. So I start walking to my own motherland in Kompong Cham.

I come to the Pol Pot checkpoint. The guard takes the letter that my brother-in-law has written, he turns it and turns it, he cannot read. So I tell him it is to say I am to go to work in another place. But he sees there is no number. My brother-in-law forgot to write a number on the letter, every letter must have a number. So the guard is angry, he say, "You are lying, you are a spy!" So I am afraid, and I cry, I say, "I am not a spy, the chief of the Pol Pot forgot to write the number", and the guard believe me and let me go. But I am afraid and I decide I will only go at night.

That night I follow the road again and I come to a river. I cannot use the bridge because there is a Pol Pot checkpoint, so I start to go down into the water. The water goes to my knees, and to my chest, and to my chin, and I am afraid because I cannot swim. But then the water starts to get shallow again, and I can climb up the other side. I stop there where there is a big tree and sun is rising and the birds are singing and the breeze is blowing in the tree and it is a beautiful day, and I miss my wife and my daughter, and I think I will go back, I miss them so much. I know the Pol Pot will catch me if I go back, but for long I stay there and think will I go on or will I go back.

That next day I hide again and come out at night and follow the road again. I have to be careful of the Pol Pot, but at night there are no people. I come to a pagoda, but there are no monks. In front of the pagoda are a lot of tombs. When I get there I meet a light, like that (pointing at the little spotlights in the restaurant ceiling), far from me. I think this is maybe Pol Pot posted there to catch people, but when I look it fly to me, and I am afraid. I sit down I close my eye. When open my eye he near me maybe two metre, and the light become the white hair, and the face is blue, had two hole, black, no eye, and the neck like a stick, and the body, and arms were sticks, but no hands, and the legs like sticks but no feet, and it is above the ground. The head is calm but the rest is moving (making a quivering motion with his hand), I cannot say in English. At that time I pray, I told him not to frighten me, that I escape from the killing, please help me to find the way to go to my village, and please take care of my wife and daughter, and at that time I stand up and I walk, and the ghost follow me about ten metre, and after I walk about 500 metre the ghost become a light and goes above and in front of me and guide me across the field across the pond across the jungle across the bamboo forest, no more the road. At daytime I sleep, I cannot see the ghost.

I reach the bank of the Mekong, there is a lot of bamboo, at that time maybe about four o'clock in the morning, not yet light, so I see the boat and take this boat, this boat full of water but not yet leak down the river. I take this boat to middle of the river, I clear the water out, I do this when I young so I know. So at this middle of the Mekong there is one island, and there are two ways (drawing a large island dividing the river into two branches). I would like to go this way, to the east, because this is my motherland, but the ghost-light is on the way near the island (the channel to the west), but I try to go east, the ghost doesn't follow me, and maybe 500 metre I have no way to go (drawing how the eastern channel turns into a dead end), so I go back, so I go the other way, and the light guide me again.

At that time of year there are so many cucumber, and the ghost guide me to the bank, and in the field they grow corn and cucumber, and I cut young corn and cucumber, and put in my bag to eat, and at that time nearly daytime, so there is small trees near the field, and I sleep. The boys bring the cows, the Pol Pot go around there, but they not enter into the small trees, I think the ghost protect me.

At night I continue across the fields, and I reach a rubber plantation, and at nighttime the ghost is guiding me. I cross the rubber plantation, maybe one night, and I know the rubber plantation is near my village. I remember that the road goes this way, (drawing a road exiting the rubber plantation in a straight line) but I like to go here (drawing a second road forking off to the right), to my village, but I lost my memory, maybe the ghost make me, I miss the road, I just walk through like this, and this the field, and this another village and pagoda, and I remember again when I see the peak of the pagoda, so I turn across the rice field, across the pond and another pond, and I go straight to my village. Later I find out there is a guard post of the Pol Pot on the straight road, if I go straight they will catch me, the ghost has found a way to escape me to my village.

In my village I find my mother my father my brothers my sisters not there, but I have my relation there and they tell the Pol Pot that I am their nephew and so I stay with my aunt. I work there and stay there from 1976 till 1978 December when my village is liberated. A lot of tanks cross my village, and Pol Pot ran away. In the commune office is a big book of names of people to be killed, my name is there, I am to be killed in January 1979.

After we are liberated I go to Mango Island to look for my wife and daughter. When I meet my wife she cry, tears stream from her eye, she tell me our daughter die because of sickness and nothing to eat. I stay in Kompong Thom till middle 1979, then I go to Phnom Penh to find a job, and after three months I bring my wife to Phnom Penh. Now I have three children, two boys and one girl. My daughter now is 18 years old.

It was six days and five nights that I was running from Kompong Thom to my village. The ghost came to me on the second night, and stayed with me till I came to the rubber plantation. When I was a child my mother told me stories of ghosts so I would not wander far, but at secondary school I learnt that the Earth goes round the Sun and I believed in science. But when I saw the ghost, I was so afraid, I had my skin like popcorn. Now when I think of the ghost, I have the same.

# The Smiling Land

Cambodia gained independence in 1953 with its traditional institutions largely intact – a Buddhist king with Brahminist trappings ruling from Phnom Penh and the people living in their villages with their monasteries and spirits. In neighbouring Vietnam, a war bogged down the French and then the Americans. Sihanouk managed to keep his country out of the turmoil to a large extent, but after his overthrow in 1970 the conflict spread to Cambodia. American bombing killed perhaps 200,000 Cambodians and ground fighting killed many more. The countryside was devastated, entire villages were wiped out and populations uprooted, the rural economy was smashed and refugees flooded the cities. When the Khmer Rouge entered Phnom Penh on 17 April 1975 they were taking over a broken country. The rule of the Khmer Rouge lasted until 7 January 1979, when Vietnamese forces entered Phnom Penh.

Nobody knows exactly how many people died between those two dates, nobody even knows what the population was at the beginning of the period or at the end, but the widely accepted estimate is about 1.8 million. Not all these deaths were the result of a deliberate intention to kill, although the Khmer Rouge leadership adopted measures that made death on a massive scale inevitable. They were socialists and revolutionaries, but more basically they were romantic nationalists in love with the distant past. Angkar, the Organization, would rebuild Angkor and Kampuchea would once more become the great nation of Suryavarman and Jayavarman, teacher to all and dependent on none, the highest expression of modernity and civilization.

The first wave of unnecessary deaths came from the conviction that cities were evil and needed to be emptied into the countryside. The inhabitants of Phnom Penh, like those of other cities and towns, were forced out without food or medicines or regard for age or sickness, hospital patients on their gurneys with drips in their arms, mothers with toddlers by their sides and infants in their arms, the old, the young, the whole and the lame.

With the cities empty the second wave of death began. Thanks to Angkar's scientific methods Cambodia would be able to grow three tons of rice per hectare in a land that had hitherto produced only one, and the surplus would be for export to China. The plan was impossible, but the people, reorganized into collectives and work brigades, were worked to exhaustion without adequate food or rest.

In September 1976 a delegation of Vietnamese women was invited to visit Cambodia and inspect progress. On their way from the border to Phnom Penh they saw many people, all dressed in black, working on what their hosts described as irrigation works, but they were not allowed to speak to them.

They were driven to Angkor. On the way they passed through Skoun, which was deserted, as were Kompong Thom and Siem Reap. In Siem Reap they asked to visit an irrigation site, and were shown one already completed. There were no people about. When they asked to see a site under active construction the visit to the countryside was cut short and they were returned to the capital.

Back in Phnom Penh they were shown a textile factory run by peasants. They were told that after only three months on the job the former farmers and revolutionaries could operate seven industrial machines simultaneously. The visitors were dubious, given that a Vietnamese worker with 12 years' experience could work only eight.

Next they were taken to see a pharmaceutical factory where workers were mixing compounds by hand. The workers were aged between twelve and fourteen. No engineers or pharmacists were needed, they were told, as Cambodian science had done away with the need for experts. The Vietnamese asked too many questions and questioned too many answers, and the visit ended in tension.

Things got worse. The Cambodians, eager to demonstrate the total nature of their revolution, explained how, in order to increase production, married women now lived separated from their husbands. But Angkar was humane, and the women were given two months' off work when they fell pregnant. A member of the Vietnamese delegation asked how the women got pregnant if they were separated from their husbands. She was told that she did not understand the problems of women.

# The Executioner's Tale

The first two waves of death – the evacuation of the cities and the imposition of a system of slave labour – can be put down to incompetence, zealotry and callousness, but they were not designed with death as their object. The deliberate killing, to which the term genocide can be applied, belongs to the third wave, when Angkar turned on itself.

How many deaths belong to the genocide? While totally reliable statistics are not available, the Documentation Centre of Cambodia has charted 20,000 mass graves – the killing fields – around the country, and estimates that they contain the remains of at least 1.1 million people and perhaps 1.5 million. All of them are the victims of execution. So if the widely accepted estimate of 1.8 million total deaths under the Khmer Rouge is accurate (it may be an underestimate, but it's unlikely to be an overestimate), then the vast majority were murder.

The murders were carried out by young men brought up to believe that taking life was the gravest of all sins. Who were they, and why did they kill?

The Documentation Centre found that villagers could often name the officials responsible for each killing field, but these individuals were almost never to be found. Professor Alexander Laban Hinton, who specializes in genocide studies, discovered a very similar result when interviewing former soldiers and cadres: they all denied ever killing anyone outside the battlefield. Finally he was put in touch with Lor, a former guard from Ponhea Yat High School on street 113 in Phnom Penh. This is now the National Genocide Museum, better known as Tuol Sleng, and under the Khmer Rouge it was the main interrogation centre for enemies of the revolution.

Hinton was told that Lor admitted to killing 400 people, but according to the few prisoners to survive Tuol Sleng the actual number was closer to 2,000. In his time at Tuol Sleng Lor "was savage like a wild animal in the forest, like a wild dog or a tiger," said one ex-prisoner who'd known him.

What does a mass killer look like? Hinton was expecting evil incarnate, but when Lor arrived for the interview he was a simple farmer with polite manners and a broad smile. He denied torturing or killing anyone, though he admitted having been a guard. He said his job had been receiving new arrivals, transporting prisoners to the killing field at Choeung Ek on the outskirts of the city, and checking names off the list as each was struck on the back of the neck with an iron bar. Personally, he never harmed a fly.

"So you never killed?"

Lor hesitated. Yes, he had killed one or two.

Hinton didn't press the point. The numbers weren't important. He asked Lor to explain why he had killed.

Lor explained that one day his boss had asked him if he had ever dared to kill a prisoner. Daring seems to be an important and deeply ambivalent quality in the Cambodian psyche. In normal life, where impulses are suppressed and the self abnegated in the interests of social harmony, daring is negative, but for those who live a little outside the mainstream – soldiers, gangsters, police – daring is desirable. For those who lack natural daring there are tattoos and amulets, and in Lor's case, there was the challenge from a superior to conform to a new set of values.

Addressing his superior respectfully, Lor admitted that he had never dared to kill.

A little way off a prisoner was kneeling in front of a guard with an iron bar. "Then," said the superior, "like your heart isn't cut off, go get that prisoner and try it once. Do it one time so I can see."

Here we have another deeply Khmer phrase, the order to act 'like your heart isn't cut off'. Possibly it means to act with courage; possibly it's an instruction to give up detachment and act in the fires of passion.

So Lor took the iron bar and struck the prisoner on the back of the neck. "When my boss asked me to do this, if I didn't do it [pause] … I couldn't refuse."

There were many thousands of Lors. Were they psychopaths, or were they 'only following orders'? Did they follow orders because they were afraid, or because they were unimaginative bureaucrats, or were they conformists, eager to fit in with fellow-murderers in a small elite for whom killing was the badge of belonging? Or did they actually believe the leaders who told them that those they killed were class enemies who had betrayed the revolution and the nation?

Khmer culture, like every other, has strong taboos against taking life, and Hinton asks how and why these taboos could have broken down.

The first part of his answer is what he calls the Principle of Disproportionate Revenge, or 'a head for an eye', and he references *Tum Teav* (see page 93) to explain it.

In Romeo and Juliet the lovers die and their grieving families are reconciled over their corpses. This would seem quite inadequate to a Cambodian audience. In *Tum Teav* the king gathers up all those responsible, plus many who are not, buries them up to their necks and runs a plough over their heads. Wrongdoing, in short, brings punishment, not reconciliation, and the punishment is gruesomely disproportionate to the crime.

The Khmer Rouge drew their fighters and cadres from the rural poor. Often these were teenagers (Angkar deliberately recruited children), and mostly they came from families and communities ripped apart by bombing and civil war. In other words, the

Khmer Rouge rank and file were unformed, uneducated, deracinated and traumatized.

They actively encouraged the new recruits to take revenge against the 'capitalists' and 'reactionary classes' who, they taught, were responsible for their suffering. A young Khmer Rouge soldier, ordered to execute 'class enemies', might therefore feel his action, and the order from his superiors, were justified in terms of Cambodian concepts of wrong-doing and revenge.

Another important element identified by Hinton is the way the Cambodian psyche manages anger. Anger is one of the 'fires' that Buddhism warns against; together with desire and delusion, it feeds the attachment to the world that is the root cause of suffering. Anger is also socially disruptive and psychically uncomfortable. Cambodian village society has erected elaborate mechanisms for its management. Folktales teach children that he who is quick to anger, who has a 'hot heart', will suffer misfortune; faced with an anger-inducing situation, the ideal is to 'calm the feeling' and 'cool the heart', restoring the same state of balance that a woman who has just given birth restores by heating her body. Anger is repressed. The result is the smile of Asia that visitors remark on, but underneath the smile lurks a capacity for quite unimaginable violence.

Buddhism discourages anger, but the Khmer Rouge encouraged it. The young cadres and fighters were educated to feel the most extreme form of 'painful anger' against American bombing and the arrogance, real or perceived, of the Phnom Penh rich. The American bombers and the rich were out of reach, so the rage was directed at Lon Nol soldiers, the police and officials, and later, when the Khmer Rouge took power, against 'class enemies' and 'traitors'. Victims arrested by Angkar and delivered up to the killing fields became the legitimate targets of 'painful anger'.

A further factor is the role of obedience and authority, which derive ultimately from the biological fact that humans are social animals and live in hierarchical bands. The famous experiments of Stanley Milgram in the 1960s are highly instructive in this regard. A teacher, T, gave instructions to a learner, L, under the direction of an experimenter, E. T believed that L was the subject of the experiment, but in fact he himself was the subject. L was set a task, and T was instructed to punish him with a harmless electric shock if he made a mistake. This, supposedly, would help L to learn. The shock increased with each successive mistake, with L first expressing pain, then pleading with T to stop. This continued until it ended in an ominous silence.

Milgram had expected that the teachers would refuse to continue at some point short of the perceived death of the learner, but most, prompted by the experimenter, continued to the end. He drew the conclusion that individuals can and will avoid personal responsibility for acts that they would normally consider morally wrong when they view themselves as no more than an agent for a higher authority. The experiment has been repeated in many different cultures with the same result.

If there is any specifically Cambodian aspect to obedience, it lies in the extremely hierarchical nature of Cambodian society. In Western societies children are all more or less equally powerless, set apart from a world of adults who are all more or less equally powerful and authoritative. The world of the Cambodian child, in contrast, is ranked.

These rankings are codified (perhaps significantly) in the language. For example, English has a single word for the second person pronoun – everyone is 'you', from a cat to a king. Not so in Cambodia. In Khmer, the pronoun varies according to the status of the person addressed, and to use the wrong word is a terrible faux pas – a farmer would not address his neighbour with the same 'you' he uses for his oxen, nor would the 'you' he uses for his neighbours be used when addressing his parents. Likewise with verbs: commoners and kings (and monks) have quite different words for actions like eating and sleeping. The closest analogy in English is to consider how animals have snouts and paws while humans have mouths and hands.

One further facet of the psychology of the Khmer Rouge killers needs mention: ritual cannibalism. Such cannibalism was not common, but it was not unknown either, and this needs to be explained.

Hinton describes an incident witnessed by a woman in a Khmer Rouge labour camp in Battambang province. A young man was condemned to be executed for digging up and eating some cassava roots – a crime because it showed selfism and a refusal to accept the standards of communal eating. The woman, daughter of a French father and Vietnamese mother, followed at a distance and watched from hiding as the condemned man was tied to a tree and blindfolded. One of the three executioners then took a knife, cut open the victim's abdomen, and removed the liver while the man was still alive. The three then cooked and ate the liver.

In this case the three executioners may well have been psychopaths – the woman describes them as arrogant and bloodthirsty. Even so, the act seems ritualistic as well as sadistic.

Cannibalism is universal. In 19th century Fiji it was normal practice to eat a dead enemy; in France in 1580, in the course of a religious pogrom, Catholic townspeople cooked and ate the internal organs of a Protestant; more recently, a U.S. soldier has described his buddies laughing at the story of a soldier in another company who ate the charred flesh of an Iraqi civilian. In each case the act was a symbolic marking of the boundary between 'us' and 'them'. Cannibalism has a spiritual dimension. For the Fijians, eating a dead warrior prevented his spirit from aiding his comrades from the other world, the French Catholics may have symbolically eaten the enemy's 'courage', and the American soldier was certainly not motivated by hunger. What did the Khmer Rouge cannibals think they were doing? Only they could answer that question, and finding an ex-Khmer Rouge willing to admit to cannibalism, much less explain himself, would be even more difficult than finding one willing to admit to mass murder. But the symbolic dimension gives a clue as to why the Cambodian cannibals chose to eat their victim's liver, since the liver, for Khmers, is the seat of daring: "I have a big liver and am not scared of anyone."

## The Religion of Angkar

Those being arrested were told, "Angkar wants to see you." Arrest led to interrogation, interrogation to confession, confession to death, for Angkar never made mistakes. Angkar had 'the eyes of a pineapple', no enemy or treachery could escape detection. And yet if someone asked who Angkar was he might be told, "Angkar is everyone; Angkar is you."

Pol Pot was Angkar. He called himself Brother Number One. There were also Brothers Number Two, Three, Four and so on. The fictive family was reinforced by marriage – Pol Pot's wife, Khieu Ponnary, head of the Association of Democratic Khmer Women and the official hostess for that team of visiting Vietnamese women, was sister to Khieu Sirith, Minister of Social Action and wife to Brother Number Three. More brothers and sons and cousins filled important posts without regard to any criterion other than blood-relatedness to the leadership.

Outside the top leadership the family, familyism, as Angkar called it, was destroyed. Husbands and wives were split up and children collectivized, private meals and private housing abolished, private property outlawed. Language itself was reformed, the single term *mitt* (comrade) replacing the multiplicity of Khmer terms for kinship and respect. All were now equal under Angkar.

Or so said the theory. In practice, local party officials were addressed as 'grandfather', or by other respectful family-based terms. Ordinary workers were reduced to the status of children, working where they were directed, assigned their sleeping places, provided with meals, even, in the time-honoured Cambodian way, told who they would marry. Angkar assumed the role and unrepayable moral debt of parents.

Other communist regimes tried to control and suppress religion, but the Khmer Rouge set out to destroy it. Monasteries were emptied, monks defrocked and sent to do useful labour or killed, temples turned into warehouses and other useful facilities. The *neak ta* were destroyed, from village shrines to the images of the great regional spirits. Festivals, both Buddhist and animist, were banned, as were alms-giving, sacred books, respectful language, religious calendars and anything that might remind the people of the old civilization. Cadres and soldiers, deriving all their power and status from Angkar, became the new priesthood. Angkar, like the Buddha, possessed perfect knowledge, and individual salvation lay in diligent obedience.

Angkar's right to rule was built on the creation of difference. Pol Pot and his circle, having studied and fully grasped Marxist-Leninism and meditated on and completely understood the reality of Cambodian society, had authority to guide the nation. The lower slopes of Angkar, where the less senior cadres dwelt, were graded according to how far its inhabitants had advanced on the path to enlightenment, and were strongly encouraged to engage in study and introspection in order to advance their lot. The population at large was divided into Base People, who were of good peasant stock and best placed to achieve revolutionary consciousness, and New People, who were not and could not.

American journalist, Elizabeth Becker, was granted an audience with Pol Pot in Phnom Penh just days before the end. She noted his quiet charisma (Cambodians would have called it his *boramey*), his aura of authority, and his fondness, shared with schoolteachers and priests, for imparting wisdom.

For over an hour she and her companions were instructed on world and Southeast Asian politics. Cambodia, Pol Pot said, was about to be invaded by the Warsaw Pact. Polish tanks and Czech infantry would roll across the rice fields to Phnom Penh, after which nothing could stop them continuing on to Bangkok, Kuala Lumpur and Singapore. Europe and America would be dragged in, a world war was possible, perhaps inevitable. NATO must come to the aid of Angkar and stop the communists in their tracks. "The man delivering the address was saying things that sounded mad."

Pol Pot was not mad in any clinical sense, but fervent believers can easily lose touch with reality. The same mentality that saw global war about to be fought over Cambodia, when applied to protecting the revolution within the borders, ordered mass death.

At the root of the killing was the creation of difference. Only the peasants possessed pure revolutionary consciousness. Town-dwellers, even former peasants who had fled there as refugees, were contaminated with false consciousness. Yet Angkar was merciful, for the attainment of correct consciousness was open to all, even New People, through study and labour.

It all sounded like a ghastly parody of Buddhist enlightenment and its attainment through meditation and merit, and perhaps it was, in part. As a boy Pol Pot spent the usual year in a Buddhist school with its rote learning and suppression of individuality, and in the early 1950s he wrote approvingly of a future democratic Cambodia which would bring back Buddhist morality; he later became an uncompromising atheist, but what he drew from his Buddhist heritage was the conviction that personal transformation was possible through discipline and the ruthless pursuit of ends.

Similarly Ta Mok, known as Brother Number Five to his colleagues or 'the butcher' to others, was once a monk at Wat Mahamontrey in Phnom Penh, where he tried to convince his fellow monks that laypeople who made donations for merit-making should instead spend their money on charity. The Buddha might well have agreed.

The pure must always have enemies, if only to validate their purity. Having created their own version of Mara's army comprising internal class enemies and external race enemies, Angkar had to deal with them, and because they were Khmer they dealt with them in a Khmer way. The interrogation records from Tuol Sleng harp constantly on the theme of strings. Traitors never acted alone, but as strings of patrons and clients. If one person was found to be a traitor, all members of that person's patron-client string had to be identified and destroyed.

They had to be destroyed, not just re-educated, because their loyalty could never be certain. The more people were killed, the greater the danger that those who remained would attempt revenge when the opportunity arose. Better, in the judgement of Angkar, to destroy. This is what lay behind the most inexplicable, the most mystifying, images from Tuol Sleng, the photos of children slated for death. They were not guilty of sins of their own, but of the sins of their fathers.

And so it went, the cycle of suspicion, purification and death continuing right up to the fall of Phnom Penh.

# 14 The Fifth Buddha

*Cambodian civilization survived the Khmer Rouge surprisingly intact. Today, however, it faces its greatest challenge ever: modernity. This is the age of the Fifth Buddha.*

## The Architect's Tale

The Fifth Buddha is waiting to be born. The signs of his coming are described in the *Put Tumniay*, a set of predictions made by the Fourth Buddha, Siddhartha Gautama, and preserved in ancient manuscripts.

The Buddha said that his teachings would last for 5,000 years. They will be years of decline, each worse than the last. At the midpoint, in the year 2500 of the Buddhist Era, the city of Kambuja will be destroyed. Roads and markets will be empty, fields will go unplanted, children will not respect parents, offerings for the gods and the ancestors will cease and the kingdom will be ruled by the enemies of religion. At the Four Arms the blood will rise as high as an elephant's belly.

Before this time a Bodhisattva called Preah Put Dammik will go to a secret place at Mount Kulen north of Angkor and enter a state of deep meditation. Indra will send Preah Pisnukar, the architect of the gods, to find him. On being awakened from his meditations, Preah Pad Dammik will retrieve hidden texts from a deep cave at Kulen and bring back Preah Koh and Preah Keo, the sacred cow and sacred gem, from Siam. He will preach to men and gods, and illness and suffering will disappear. Finally he will consecrate two kings who will rule over the land of the Khmers in keeping with *dhamma*, and usher in the age of the Fifth Buddha.

In the 1980s the *Put Tumniay* was widely believed to have predicted Pol Pot, but today more than half the population is too young to have ever known the Khmer Rouge and the prophecy is held to refer to the current age.

In the early 1990s a prophet calling himself Tapas (pronounced *tapoh*) emerged. A tapas is a holy hermit. They are frequently depicted in monasteries and at holy shrines as elderly men with long beards, their hair piled up in a topknot and wearing a tiger-skin robe. This Tapas was young and had no beard, but he dressed in a hermit's robe and claimed to have received superhuman powers through long and strenuous meditations in the jungles on the borders between Thailand and Burma. Burma is renowned for similar figures called Zawgyis, alchemists who seek to transform stones into gold, and it's not impossible that the Cambodian Tapas had studied magic with the Burmese Zawgyis.

Tapas made the claim that he was able to transform clay into stone. He built a temple out of clay at Kien Svay, south of Phnom Penh, with towers and staring faces on the roof. His magic knowledge would turn it to stone, he said, just as the Architect of the Gods had done when building Angkor Wat. Possibly the faces were his own. He also buried wood and clay statues that would turn into bronze after being buried for three years. This eventually proved his undoing.

He became famous. Supporters in America were extremely generous and he built himself a villa, which was not really in keeping with the lifestyle of a holy hermit, and promised that when his clay temple turned to stone he would usher in the age of the Fifth Buddha.

Eventually the day came for the clay and wood statues to be dug up. A huge crowd gathered, but Tapas was nowhere to be seen. It was the end, and he was no longer taken seriously.

Or almost. I visited him in 2008 with my friend Davuth, the one who failed to see King Sihanouk in the moon, and he was still there, in a concrete temple that looked quite sturdy. We waited patiently while he attended to some well-dressed Khmer Americans who had come all the way from Long Beach to help arrange a forthcoming fund-raising visit to the United States. While we waited I looked around. Baroque hardly does justice to Tapas' architectural sense. There were grottoes and statues and swags of banners, and the assorted nick-nacks that so often seem to be essential to this approach to the supernatural.

When he saw us he was charming, and gave us the usual blessings. Davuth was polite at the time, but later he was angry and said Tapas was a fraud who made the Khmer people into an international laughing-stock. Personally I got the impression that Tapas believed in himself completely.

## Religion in an Age of Plenty

Since the mid-1990s Cambodia's economy has grown at over seven per cent each year, making the 21st century an age of plenty.

The garment industry is now Cambodia's biggest foreign income earner, with exports worth five billion dollars a year. The workforce is made up overwhelmingly of young women from the villages, thrown into a community of a type never before seen in Cambodia – an all-female world of repetitive and regimented work, long hours with little time off (quite often the factories don't respect the big national holidays like Pchum Ben, the owners being mostly Chinese) and, perhaps most importantly, no connection to the past or to community.

The work is hard and stressful, but Cambodian girls are brought up to be dutiful. They don't complain, they don't disobey their elders and they work diligently at their tasks. But they're not happy. How are the newly-minted factory girls to make their unhappiness known?

In October 2012, 250 girls fainted at the Chinese-owned Anful Garment Factory at Bavet near the Vietnamese border. They were rushed to hospital, where the doctors were mystified but gave them an intravenous glucose drip and a night in bed, then sent them back to work.

The production line no sooner started up than another round of mass fainting broke out. This time a *neak ta* told the Anful management what was wrong. Speaking through one of the girls, he said that the factory was on his land, and he was very, very angry because he hadn't been given proper respect. He wanted an apology for the neglect he'd suffered, and proper offerings.

At this point I begin to feel a twinge of sympathy for the Chinese owners of Anful, because the big Western buyers will switch suppliers from Cambodia to Bangladesh in a heartbeat, and while labour unions can be negotiated with and stiff-armed if necessary, spirits must be treated with circumspection.

A Buddhist ceremony was held at the factory, in which the factory owners donated 30 cases of bottled water, two cases of Coca Cola, fresh coconuts, cigarettes, bathrobes, toiletries, razors, tea, sugar and soap to the chief monk. The abbot splashed the workers with holy water and chanted a prayer to appease the *neak ta*, who received offerings of rice spirits and raw chicken.

Mass faintings are endemic in the garment factories. Usually poor ventilation is blamed, or poor nutrition, but in fact there seems to be no identifiable physical cause. About a third of the cases involve appearances by *neak ta*. Sometimes they merely win the girls a few days off work, but other times they open the way for labour unions to negotiate with management and lead to improved wages and conditions.

The age of plenty is an age of greed. Forests are being logged, rivers are being dammed and the natural world comprehensively trampled. But of all the ills facing contemporary Cambodia, land-grabbing is perhaps the most comprehensive. Over two million hectares (five million acres) of village land have been seized and more than 400,000 people displaced as commercial rubber and sugar plantations replace rice land, and in the city whole communities are being evicted to make way for forests of luxury condominiums which one must doubt will ever be inhabited. Stories of protests, jailings and conflicts between protesters and riot police dominate the newspapers. Corruption is rampant, legal avenues of redress are largely useless and the dispossessed lack the resources to fight the *neak thom*.

Yet while Cambodia is an oligarchic kleptocracy, it is also a democracy. As a democracy it's far from perfect, but people are free to demonstrate in the streets, and they do. They do so at some risk, however: rallies are routinely broken up by the paramilitary, protest leaders are arrested and jailed by courts that are at the beck and call of the country's rulers, and activists and journalists are occasionally murdered.

As in the garment factories, the spirit world plays a part on the side of the oppressed. On Thursday, 12 June 2013, several hundred demonstrators gathered at Preah Ang Doung Kar. Watched by riot police in combat gear they prayed for the protection of the spirits before moving on to the Ministry of Justice, the Supreme Court and the National Assembly. There they burnt life-sized effigies of a judge, a prosecutor and a lawyer, whose pockets were stuffed with Chinese ghost money symbolizing corruption. They placed a black magic curse on their enemies with crucified chickens, the favourite offering of Yeay Tep of Siem Reap. "I want the government and involved institutions to help solve the problems of the poor people with land and housing," said one protester. "We want the Justice Ministry and all involved ministries to intervene and drop charges against the activists on land, forestry, natural resources and housing."

Political activism has also emerged among monks, who are supporting the wage campaigns of the garment workers, calling for the protection of villages and forests, and sometimes joining in overtly political campaigns in support of opposition parties.

The Independent Monks Network for Social Justice claims a membership of 5,000, a tenth of all monks in the country. Most are in Phnom Penh, which is also the focus of demonstrations and activism generally. Behind the activist monkhood lies the rapid rise of social media (I have yet to meet a monk without a smartphone and a Facebook account), the equally rapid shift in demographics (most monks are young) and the fact that the majority of monks in the capital are from poor rural families and hence well aware of the issues affecting the villages.

In December 2014, 600 monks and activists organized a march from six different points around the country to Phnom Penh. The march, held to mark World Human Rights Day, had highly emotive echoes of a famous series of peace marches organized in the early 1990s by a revered monk called Ghosananda.

The authorities, unhappy with activists in general, are doubly unhappy with activist monks. The Supreme Patriarchs of the two sects promptly issued a statement forbidding monks from taking part, and police ordered all monasteries to shut their gates on activists seeking shelter in their compounds at night.

Activist monks are regularly defrocked (expelled from the monkhood) and imprisoned, and the Supreme Patriarch is calling for monks to be banned from joining in politics and from voting. Nevertheless, organizations such as Amnesty International, not to mention domestic society, vigorously defend the right of monks and others to oppose injustice. Images spread by social media of monks being beaten up by riot police potentially alienate the broader population.

All these can be, and are, justified as in keeping with the Buddha's teachings. "What is the definition of politics?" one monk asked rhetorically. "According to the Khmer Dictionary ... it is a method to lead a group of people to a specific goal. By this definition I feel that Buddhism is also politics, because Buddhism leads the people towards happiness and peace."

## The Great Migration

The great worldwide migration from the countryside to the city has hardly begun in Cambodia. Eighty per cent of the population still lives in villages, which means that village religion is the religion of the people.

Village religion is based around the spirits and the monastery. The spirits enforce morality and good behaviour. "Honour the ancestors and thy father and mother," says the neak ta, "or I shall strike thee down with severe stomach cramps." "Thou shalt not have premarital sex," say the meba, "and nor shalt thou mistreat the cow that is thine," say the mrieng kongveal. "Learn from my terrible example," says the arp. "Don't be vain, don't try to stay young forever, don't be a slovenly housewife."

The monastery backs up the spirits. "Do no harm," says the Buddha, and the village *kru* does no harm, or else she runs the risk of being mistaken for a sorcerer, for which the penalty, all too often, is death. "Honour the dead, and also your parents and ancestors" say the spirits, and at New Year and Pchum Ben the monastery offers the means to do so.

The city is something new in Cambodia. There's only one: Phnom Penh. Sihanoukville, Battambang and Siem Reap don't come close to rivalling it. The capital of Cambodia is a phenomenon, growing faster than almost every other city in East Asia according to the World Bank. It sprawls over 160 ill-serviced square kilometres (62 sq miles), and its population has doubled in less than 20 years.

Almost no city-dweller is more than a generation removed from the village, yet the city has its own dynamic and imposes new ways of living – crowds, jobs, employment relations, social media, and exposure to Western and Sino-Japanese culture. What difference does city life make to Cambodian religion?

Of the three major national festivals, the New Year, Pchum Ben and the Water Festival, the first two remain village-based. Everyone in Phnom Penh goes home, and home is the village. The third festival, the Water Festival in November, is a Phnom Penh festival, although smaller versions are held throughout the country. All three are thriving.

*An offering to the spirit of a racing boat at the Water Festival in Siem Reap.*

Among the spirits, the protective *chumneang pteah* (house-guardian) and *tevoda* (heavenly protectors) and the wish-granting *mrieng kongveal* (spirit-cowherds) have all come to the city. So has the *preah phum*, the owner of the land, as the patron of non-domestic property. Preah Torani, the earth-goddess, along with her avatars as crocodile and *naga*, remains potent – when the statue of the two Techo horsemen on the Riverside opposite Wat Ounalom was inaugurated the crocodile-god was first asked for permission to disturb the soil, in accordance with tradition. And of course the Riverside shrine continues to attract those seeking blessings and protection.

The village *neak ta* have not made the transition. No sangkat (the lowest level of urban local government) or khan (the next highest level) has a *neak ta* shrine. Daun Penh is the *neak ta* of the city, but she doesn't function in the same way as a village *neak ta* – she doesn't enforce norms of behaviour, and the gardens around her shrine are infamous as the haunt of prostitutes, which would be unimaginable in a village.

Since the spirits traditionally made their displeasure known through illness, the growth of modern medicine and the spread of clinics and doctors should, one would expect, have a profound effect on spirit belief and magic, but in fact it doesn't seem to. People go to the clinic or doctor, but they still consult the *kru*. Given the hit-or-miss nature of Cambodian medicine this could continue into the foreseeable future. And modern medicine has nothing to say about increasing one's store of *bonn*, or reducing *kamm*, or dealing with death and the dead.

City life encourages materialism, and Cambodians are no less eager than anyone else to embrace the good life. Buddhism, in contrast, teaches that material goods are illusions and snares, and that salvation will come through voluntary poverty, study and meditation. The monks I met were mainly poor country boys, and almost all were monks only as a means to an end. Almost all, but not quite all: some monks are genuinely committed to a life of study and meditation, and others, possibly ten per cent, are involved in social activism. The top level of the hierarchy is firmly welded to the political order, but this is nothing new – the Sangha has never been independent of political power.

Valentine's Day is a Western innovation that has become immensely popular in modern urban Cambodia, and it cuts directly across traditional Khmer values. Khmer girls are romantic, but Khmer teenage boys, like teenage boys everywhere, tend to confuse love and sex. In 2012 Sivann Botum, Secretary of State for Women's Affairs, told *Kyodo News* that her ministry had produced a video to educate youth on the proper

*Daun Penh at Wat Phnom.*

ways of celebrating Valentine's Day.

Schools have banned the sale of flowers outside their gates in the lead-up to Valentine's Day, and police have put plain-clothes officers in guesthouses and hotels to check on the ages of guests.

"I beg women to maintain our Khmer traditions," said Sivann Botum, "because virginity is very important."

## The Dance of Modernity

A modern state has a professional and efficient bureaucracy to collect taxes and implement the state's policies. The modern state is participatory, meaning that society is organized and represented in the formation of policy, with the result that the state's taxation and spending is regarded as legitimate. The state itself is under the rule of law, meaning that its actions are not arbitrary and can be appealed in the courts.

Cambodia is none of these things. Cambodia is not a modern state. Getting states like Cambodia from pre-modern to modern – the process of democratization – is one of the great conundrums facing the world.

One of the biggest hurdles to democracy in Cambodia is khsae, the organization of society and politics by patronage. Patronage not merely condones corruption, it mandates it, since it depends on the generation and distribution of benefits.

The United States and Britain also once had political networks based on patronage. It was ended in these countries through the combined pressure of new social classes, the professional middle classes, seeking employment based on merit and education, and business interests that valued efficient and transparent administration. In Cambodia today the growth of the economy is generating similar new classes, based on education, enterprise and personal merit. The end of patronage is not inevitable, but the scope for these classes to pursue their interests through the electoral system exists, highly imperfect though that system is.

When religion fails, people are left with a return to an imagined past, like Tapas, or the attractions of an entirely new world.

The new religion is Christianity, specifically the evangelical version. Nobody really knows how many Christians there are in Cambodia, but probably not many – the U.S. State Department's annual report on international religious freedom reckons they probably comprise about two per cent of the population. Nevertheless, foreign evangelical churches are actively seeking converts and claim that their numbers are growing rapidly.

For some Cambodians, the Christian God offers precisely the same benefits as the *mrieng kongveal*: "I prayed for a motorbike and my parents bought me one but it was old and I prayed again and it was stolen and God knew my will and one of the Christians in the church bought me a new one," to quote a Christian interviewed by the *Phnom Penh Post*. Prayer operates like magic, and materialism has deep roots in the Khmer psyche. But for others, and probably most, the motivation is not so crass. The churches offer a sense of community and mutual help that are missing in traditional Cambodian society, both in the village and the city. I heard this from many of the Christians I interviewed, young and old. The Cambodian village is not a strong community, the city is even colder, and the church offers genuine fellowship, plus a faith that binds its members together and teaches an ethical doctrine that's almost completely absent from Buddhism.

Conversion to Christianity comes at a cost. To be Khmer is to be Buddhist, and to cease to be Buddhist is almost an act of treason. Even more, Christianity has a reputation as a religion that teaches disrespect for parents, attacking one of the foundations of Khmer society. It comes as a surprise and a relief to young would-be converts to find that they aren't expected to turn their backs on their families.

They do, however, very frequently turn their backs on the festivals that bind the individual to the family and the family to the community, notably Khmer New Year and Pchum Ben. The churches themselves, by and large, have no policy or teaching on this, but many individual converts find themselves unable in conscience to attend the wat or to take part in the rituals, especially those that involve paying respect to Buddha-images and monks. Christians therefore tend to form their own communities and lead a life apart from the other villagers. In the long run, if Christianity builds a critical mass, it has the potential to pose a real threat to traditional Cambodian life.

## The King's Tale

The role of the king under French protection was to be a complaisant puppet. King Norodom, however, proved difficult: he kept agreeing to do what the French wanted, then failing to follow though. After two decades the French had had enough. Early one June morning in 1884 the Governor of Indo-China (who had the very un-French name of Thomson) forced his way into Norodom's bed-chamber and made him sign over his power to gather taxes, without which no government can function. Norodom resisted for three hours, but the consequences of not signing were clear: the palace was surrounded by French troops and three French gunboats sat in the river outside.

Norodom, humiliated, retreated into opium dreams in the palace, and his two successors, his brother Sisowath and Sisowath's son Monivong, were happy to follow his example. Sihanouk, who had more power than any Khmer monarch in centuries,

154 I 14 THE FIFTH BUDDHA

called them the parrot kings, but Sihanouk brought Cambodia the Khmer Rouge. Today the monarchy is purely symbolic, and the power to rule rests with the Prime Minister.

But the king remained and remains the centre of the mandala. At the annual Ploughing Ceremony he guides the royal plough, after which the oxen are led to seven bowls containing water, wine, rice, maize, sesame, corn and grass to predict the fortunes of the coming year. (If they choose water there will be plentiful rain, if rice the crop will be good, but wine or beans mean disaster.) The Water Festival is more than a three-day boat race, for it involves certain ceremonies only the king can preside over, and the New Year likewise requires his participation. Even Pchum Ben has certain unique royal ceremonies, conducted at the riverbank by Preah Ang Doung Kar. Given this, it's hardly surprising that Lon Nol had to be forced at gunpoint to dethrone the sacred king. (The man who held the gun was Sihanouk's cousin Sirik Matak, who felt that he, not Sihanouk, should have been on the throne.)

King Sihamoni can trace his ancestry back to Jayavarman VII and even beyond, to the prince from India who married the daughter of the *naga* king. His palace looks out over the Four Rivers, reflecting the rivers that flow from sacred Lake Anotatta at the summit of Meru, where Queen Maya bathed before the Bodhisattva entered her womb. In the palace are the sacred regalia, including Preah Khan, the sacred sword that protects the kingdom, and the statue of his ancestor Norodom in the form of the Fifth Buddha. Kingship, in short, is surrounded by symbolic meaning, and every Cambodian understands the story.

When a king dies he is cremated on a funeral pyre lit by his eldest son, as is any other Cambodian. Sihanouk lit the pyre for his father Suramarit in 1960, and his own pyre was lit by his son Sihamoni, assisted by Queen Mother Norodom Monineath and the Supreme Patriarchs of the two Buddhist orders.

Or so the official record shows. But speaking later at an inauguration ceremony at Preah Sihamoni Reachea Buddhist University, the Prime Minister revealed that all four attempts to put a candle to the funeral pyre failed, because the King Father didn't want to leave his children (i.e., the Cambodian people). "The Queen Mother said that the King Father [Sihanouk] waits for Samdech Prime Minister." It was only when Hun Sen held the candle that the flames caught and spread.

# Works Consulted

## Newspapers and websites

'Magic, curses and affairs of the heart', Charlotte McDonald-Gibson and Lon Nara, *Cambodia Daily*, Friday 11 October 2002.

'Hit-and-run kills 3', Khouth Sophak Chakrya and Claire Slattery, *Phnom Penh Post*, 4 March 2013

'Hit-and-run driver to be out in weeks', Buth Reaksmeay Kongkea, *Phnom Penh Post*, 13 June 2013

'Hun Sen's relative admits to hit-and-run', Chrann Chamroeun, *Phnom Penh Daily*, 13 August 2008.

'Jubilant crowds celebrate at hill of human sacrifice', Liam Cochrane, *Phnom Penh Post*, 1 July, 2005.

'Factory boss tried for crumpling moon picture', Mom Kunthear, *Phnom Penh Post*, 26 October 2012

'Explaining the Factory Faintings', Julia Wallace and Neou Vannarin, *Cambodia Daily*, November 23, 2012 and 'Workers of the World, Faint!Julia Wallace, *International New York Times*, January 17

'A vigilant Valentine's,' May Titthara and Shane Worrell, *Phnom Penh Post*, 14 February 2012.

'"Miracle" cremation: PM Hun Sen', by Meas Sokhchea, *Phnom Penh Post*, 15 February 2013

'Whither Cambodia's Monarchy?' Parameswaran Ponnudurai, Radio Free Asia.

## Books and articles

ANON (A French Army-Surgeon). 1900. *Untrodden Fields of Anthropology: Observations on the Esoteric Manners and Customs of Primitive Peoples*, vol.1, privately re-issued by the American Anthropological Society, New York.

ANG, C. 1988. *The Place of Animism Within Popular Buddhism in Cambodia: The Example of the Monastery* (*Asian Folklore. Studies*, vol.47 no. 1:35–41). aefek.free.fr/iso_album/angchoulean1.pdf

ANG, C. 2004. *Brah Ling*.

BECKER, E. 1998. *When the War was Over*.

BERTRAND, D. 2001. The Names and Identities of the Boramey Spirits Possessing Cambodian Mediums, *Asian Folklore Studies*, vol.60, p.31-47.

BUNNAG, J. 1991. The Way of the Monk and the Way of the World: Buddhism in Thailand, Laos and Cambodia, *The World Of Buddhism*, ed. H. Bechert and R. Gombert.

CHAN, V. 2013. *Wat Phnom: Guide to Art and Architecture*.

CHANDLER, D. 1971. Royally Sponsored Human Sacrifices in Nineteenth Century Cambodia: The Cult of Nak Ta Me Sa (Mahisasuramardini) at Ba Phnom. *Journal of the Siam Society*. vol.62/2:207-222

CHIGAS, G. 2005. *Tum Teav: A Translation and Interpretation of a Khmer Literary Classic.*

CONZE, E. 1993. *Buddhism: A Short History.*

DAVIS, E. W. 2013. Beginning a Sketch of Accumulation by Dispossession in Contemporary Cambodia. *Fieldsights - Episcope, Cultural Anthropology.* Online, 2013.

DIBIASIO, J. 2013. *The Story of Angkor.*

DIM, D. (no date) *The Hungry Ghost for Sandwiches.*

EAR, S. 2012. *Aid Dependence in Cambodia: How Foreign Assistance Undermines Democracy.*

EBIHARA, M. M. 1968. *Svay, A Khmer Village in Cambodia.* (PhD dissertation in the collection of the Hun Sen Library, Royal University of Phnom Penh.)

ETCHESON, C. 2008. The Number: Quantifying Crimes Against Humanity in Cambodia, *Mekong Net*, October 6, 2008.

GOMBRICH, R. 1991. The Buddhist Way, *The World Of Buddhism*, ed. H. Bechert and R. Gombrich.

GUTHRIE, E. 2004. *A Study of the Buddhist Earth Deity in Mainland Southeast Asia*, PhD thesis submitted to the University of Canterbury, Christchurch NZ.

HARVEY, G. 2013. *Animism: Respecting the Living World.*

HARVEY, P. 2012. *An Introduction to Buddhism: Teachings, History and Practices.*

HODGES, L. 2012. *Reincarnating Knowledge: Training the Lay Buddhist Priesthood of Khmer Achars in Cambodia.* World Faiths Development Dialogue

HINTON, A. L. 2004. *Why Did They Kill? Cambodia in the Shadow of Genocide.*

HOLT, J. C. 2012. Caring for the Dead Ritually in Cambodia, *Southeast Asian Studies*, vol.1, no.1, April, pp. 3–75.

JACOBSEN, T. 2012. Being Broh: The Good, the Bad, and the Successful Man in Cambodia, *Men and Masculinities in Southeast Asia*, ed. M. Ford and L. Lyons.

JACOBSEN, T. 2008. *Lost Goddesses: The Denial of Female Power in Cambodian History.*

JACOBSEN, T., and STUART-FOX, M. 2013. *Power and Political Culture in Cambodia* (Asian Research Institute Working Paper, Series No. 200)

JERMSAWATDI, P. 1979. *Thai Art with Indian Influences.*

KENT, A. 2008. The Recovery of the King, *People of Virtue: Reconfiguring Religion,Power and Moral Order in Cambodia Today*, ed. A. Kent, D. P. Chandler.

KIERNAN, B. 2008. *The Pol Pot Regime.*

LEDGERWOOD, J. 2008. Ritual in 1990s Cambodian Political Theatre: New Songs at the Edge of the Forest, *Songs at the Edge of the Forest: Essays on Cambodia, History, and Narrative in Honor of David Chandler*, ed. A. R. Hansen and J. Ledgerwood.

MEHTA, H. C., and MEHTA, J. B. 2013. *Strongman: The Extraordinary Life of Hun Sen.*

MIZERSKI, J. 2013. *Finale: The Royal Cremations of Norodom and Norodom Sihanouk, Kings of Cambodia.*

MULLER, G. 2006. *Colonial Cambodia's 'Bad Frenchmen': The Rise of French Rule and the Life of Thomas Caraman, 1840-87.*

NOREN-NILSSON, A., Performance as (Re)incarnation: The Sdech Kan Narrative, *Journal of Southeast Asian Studies,* vol.44, no.1.

OSBORNE, M. 2014. Buddhist Monks and Political Activism in Cambodia, *The Interpreter,* 29 September.

PHIM, N. 2007. *Reflections of a Khmer Soul.*

PYM, C. 1961. *Mistapim in Cambodia.*

RAVASCO, G. 2006. *Towards a Christian Pastoral Approach to Cambodian Culture.*

SHORT, P. 2004. *Pol Pot.*

STENCEL, R., GIFFORD, F., and MORON, E. 1976. Astronomy and Cosmology at Angkor Wat, *Science,* 23 July, vol.193, no.4250, pp.281-287.

STRANGIO, S. 2014. *Hun Sen's Cambodia.*

STUART-FOX, M., and REEVE, P. 2011. Symbolism in City Planning in Cambodia, *Journal of the Siam Society,* vol.99.

THIERRY, S, *The Khmer.*

THIERRY, S. 1993. Southeast Asia, *Asian Mythologies* ed. Y. Bonnefoy.

THOMPSON, A. 2005. *Calling the Souls: A Cambodian Ritual Text.*

THOMPSON, A. 2006. Buddhism in Cambodia: Rupture and Continuity, *Buddhism in World Cultures: Comparative Perspectives,* ed. S. C. Berkwitz.

THOMPSON, A. 1998. Lost and Found: The Stupa, the Four Faced Buddha, and the Seat of Royal Power, *Southeast Asian Archaeology*

U SILANANDA. 2011. *Vipassana Meditation Instructions.*

ZHOU, D. 2007. *A Record of Cambodia, the Land and its People,* translated with introduction and notes by P. Harris, foreword by D. Chandler.

# Index

Abhidhamma 66, 67, 108
Achar 70, 71, 72, 81,
   100, 102, 106, 108,
   111, 117, 118
Alexander Laban Hinton,
   Prof. 137
Ananda 14, 15, 98
Ang Chan 55, 92
Angkor Wat, 17, 21, 28,
   119, 120, 124, 145
Animism 25, 43, 102
Apsaras 11, 16, 18, 21, 32
Arak 26, 35, 37, 104
Architect's Tale 144
Arp 36, 37, 74, 148
Ashley Thompson, Prof. 130
Asura 11, 16, 71
Atman 25
Ayutthaya 55
Ba Phnom 89, 128
Banteay Meanchey 37, 56
Battambang 56, 72, 74, 92,
   93, 109, 110, 140, 149
Benares 13
Blessed One 14
Bodhi Tree 10, 11, 12,
   28, 35, 55, 58, 89
Bodhisattva
   7, 120, 122, 144, 154
Bon sak 44
Bong thom 45
Bonn 45, 47, 69, 72, 109, 115,
   123, 142, 150
Boramey 26, 44, 61, 74,
   85, 87, 88, 94, 95, 96, 97
Brahma 8, 11, 12, 13
Brahmin 7, 12, 13, 21,
   22, 51, 53, 130
Bray 32, 35, 88, 102
Cham 23, 45, 51, 53,
   56, 97, 114, 130, 133
Buddha 6–15, 16, 22, 25, 31,
   32, 37, 43, 49, 50, 55, 60,
   62, 64, 65, 66, 70, 71, 72,
   78, 81, 84, 87, 88, 96, 98,
   99, 100, 107, 116, 117, 119,
   120, 122, 125, 130, 142, 143
Cham Muslims 23
Champa 51, 110
Chanthy 38, 39, 40
Chenla 109
Chey Aschar 92, 93
Christopher Pym 105

Chumneang pteah
   34, 35, 39, 40, 62, 80,
   81, 82, 83, 100, 150
Dam Po 28, 29, 31
Daun chi 34, 60, 71, 72, 107
Daun Chi Chan Sopheap 72
Daun Mao 97
Daun Penh 50, 96, 124, 150
Daun Phann 93, 94, 95, 96, 97
Davan 112, 113, 114, 115
Devatas 11, 12, 16, 21
Dey Leou 45
Dhamma 14, 22, 24,
   60, 99, 107, 145
Dhammapul 45
Dhammayutika 56
Dukkha 22, 25, 68, 69, 93
Eightfold Path, 23
Eng Sok 34
Etienne Aymonier 94
Eveline Poree-Maspero 108
Executioner's Tale 137
Festival of Hungry Ghosts 115
Fifth Buddha 119, 126, 128,
   144, 145–154
First Ghost's Tale 112
First Nun's Tale 72
Garudas 11, 18, 21, 80
Georges Coedes 21
Great Migration 148
Hau Pralung 82, 99
Himeanakas 52
Hindush 22
Hun Chea 48
Hun Sen 33, 44, 45, 46,
   48, 129, 130, 131, 154
Hungry Ghosts 11, 111, 115
Im Kim Ly 83, 84
Independence Monument
   46, 61, 130, 131
Indra 8, 11, 12, 13, 17,
   18, 21, 52, 54, 87, 144
Indus River 22
Jainism, 22
Jambu 16, 17
Jambudvipa 7, 16
Jayavarman VII 45, 53,
   105, 119, 122, 154
Jesus 6
Kai 128
Kalpa 17
Kamadhenu 18
Kambu 51

Kambuja 51, 144
Kamm 41, 43, 44, 69,
   72, 73, 114, 150
Kampong 45, 114
Kampong Cham 45, 114
Kampuchea Krom 62, 122
Kampuchea Surin 122
Kandal Province 34, 62, 70, 110
Kapilavastu 7, 8, 9
Kaundinya 51, 52
Kbal Mohaprom 76, 77
Kdey Takoy 70
Keam Piseth Narita 46
Keng Brasath 109
Keosupha 74
Khleang Moeung 87, 92, 93
Khsae 44, 152
Kim Sam 68
King Ang Duong 56
King Ibrahim 126
King Jayavarman VII 53, 119
King Monivong 128
King Norodom 89, 124,
   126, 128, 130, 153
King Ponhea Yat
   53, 68, 124, 125, 130, 137
King Preah Ket Mealea 21
King Rama 55, 93, 94
King Ramathipadi I 126
King Sihanouk 45, 72, 87,
   109, 128, 145
Kmouch 111, 113, 114, 115
Koki tree 35, 124
Koma Pich 61
Komlang 44
Kompong Cham 97, 133
Kompong Thom 132, 135, 136
Kon Aeuy Madai Arp 36
Kongma 81, 82
Koraka Tevi 77, 78
Kratie province 109
Krong Bali 49, 50
Kru 26, 29, 32, 35, 37, 38, 39,
   62, 85, 87, 88, 94, 106, 109,
   113, 114, 115, 149, 150
Kru arak 26, 35, 37
Kru boramey
   26, 37, 85, 87, 94, 115
Kru khmer 26, 37
Lake Anotatta 7, 17, 154
Lekhena 112, 113
Leng Sophoan 78, 79
Leung Sak 78

Dedication
To Socheat Cheng, my interpreter and guide, and above all to the wonderful, warm-hearted Khmer people.


First published in the United Kingdom in 2015 by John Beaufoy Publishing Ltd,
11 Blenheim Court, 316 Woodstock Road, Oxford OX2 7NS, England
www.johnbeaufoy.com

10 9 8 7 6 5 4 3 2 1

ISBN 978-1-909612-52-5

Designed by Gulmohur Press, New Delhi
Project management by Rosemary Wilkinson

Captions to chapter opening photos:
p.6 Birth of the Buddha, painting in a rural monastery; p.16 Angkor Wat; p.27 Daun Penh, legendary founder of Phnom Penh; p.41 Earth-spirits; p.49 Preah Torani; p.58 Spirit flag in a country temple; p.68 The abbot of Wat Sarawan monastery, Phnom Penh; p.76 Tevodas; p.85 Wrist threads for protection; p.98 Spirit flag at Wat Ounalom, Phnom Penh; p.111 Monks receiving offerings, Wat Lanka, Phnom Penh; p.119 Lotus buds to invite the spirits; p.132 Khmer Rouge victim, Tuol Sleng genocide museum, Phnom Penh; p.144 Statue of the fifth Buddha, Wat Phnom, Phnom Penh.

Printed and bound in Malaysia by Times Offst (M) Sdn. Bhd.


Acknowledgements
Many people helped me with this book; my thanks go to all of them, and especially to His Excellency Hang Sovann, Advisor to the Committee for National and International Festivals, who explained many obscure matters to me, to Margaret Bywater of the Hun Sen Library of the Royal University of Phnom Penh, who introduced me to the works of Christopher Pym, and to the *Cambodia Daily* and *Phnom Penh Post* for permission to quote extensively from articles.